W9-BOM-533

Keeping Watch

Jill,
Best wishes to a fellow Knitter,
Enjoy the book !
Kathy Sletto

KEEPING WATCH

30 Sheep, 24 Rabbits, 2 Llamas,
1 Alpaca, and a Shepherdess
with a Day Job

KATHRYN A. SLETTO

BOREALIS
BOOKS

Borealis Books is an imprint of the Minnesota Historical Society Press.
www.borealisbooks.org

© 2010 by the Minnesota Historical Society. All rights reserved. No part of this book may be used or reproduced in any manner whatsoever without written permission, except in the case of brief quotations embodied in critical articles and reviews. For information, write to Borealis Books, 345 Kellogg Blvd. W., St. Paul, MN 55102-1906.

The Minnesota Historical Society Press is a member of the Association of American University Presses.

Manufactured in the United States of America

10   9   8   7   6   5   4   3   2   1

♾ The paper used in this publication meets the minimum requirements of the American National Standard for Information Sciences—Permanence for Printed Library Materials, ANSI Z39.48-1984.

International Standard Book Number
ISBN: 978-0-87351-770-6 (cloth)

Library of Congress Cataloging-in-Publication Data
Sletto, Kathryn A. (Kathryn Albertson)
    Keeping watch : 30 sheep, 24 rabbits, 2 llamas, 1 alpaca, and a shepherdess with a day job / Kathryn A. Sletto.
        p. cm.
    ISBN 978-0-87351-770-6 (cloth : alk. paper)
    1. Sletto, Kathryn A. (Kathryn Albertson)
    2. Shepherds—United States—Biography.
    3. Women shepherds—United States—Biography.
    4. Women executives—United States—Biography.
    5. Animal culture—United States—Anecdotes. I. Title.
    SF375.32.S565A3 2010
    636.30092—dc22
    [B]

Photograph page ii: ©iStockphoto.com/GlobalP. All others, Christopher Sletto.

Publication of this book was supported in part with funds provided by the Ken and Nina Rothchild Fund for Business History and Women's History.

For Rose

Contents

3   Gidget, the giddy camel

8   The spinning wheel

14   Something's got to give

18   Shepherdess

25   Lamb Chop

36   Tux

40   Whiplash

43   Tony

48   Hunting and gathering

52   The office

60   Ted, Mr. Johnson, and the flood

73   Rosie's twins

82   Ragnar and Mrs. Harris

91   Shearing

97   Egg-sucking dog

105   Summer vacation

112   A thief in the night

115   Lamb kill

119 Marketing

122 Emma the rabbit, armed and dangerous

130 Whiplash goes to town

133 Identity crisis

136 Elmo the bird

145 The nature of sheep

151 Drought

153 Coyotes, Mack Dawg, and Camilla

158 Tux and Daisy

160 The county fair

172 Mack Dawg's very bad day

181 September

186 Steve, the wayward rabbit

196 Ruth and Esther

207 Conclusion

211 Keeping watch

216 Epilogue

219 Acknowledgments

Keeping Watch

Gidget, the giddy camel

Their wide-eyed looks of horror said it all. They sat in stunned silence at the kitchen table, newspapers and homework forgotten. This was not the reaction I expected from my husband and twelve-year-old son. I had rushed home, eager to share my exciting news. The news involved a camel—the only camel in North Dakota, in fact. And it was for sale.

At the time, I worked as a freelance grant writer and grants management consultant for several small towns in western Minnesota, including Browns Valley. The Browns Valley office staff provided me with a never-ending supply of good-natured gossip, local folklore, and other benefits not the least of which was gainful employment. Linda, the city clerk, and her assistant, Candy, kept an eye out for things that might interest me. They knew of my passion for animals and the motley assortment of pets masquerading as livestock on my family's small farm near Alexandria, eighty miles to the east. Whether it was the city council member who raised exotic animals or the two-for-one deal on cat neutering at the local vet clinic, the two women kept me up to date on community news and events.

But the girls had outdone themselves this time. "Look at this," said Candy. "There's a camel for sale. It's just a young one, and her owners have to sell her."

Candy held out a clipping from a regional farm journal. Sure enough, there it was: an ad for a camel for sale. "The only camel in North Dakota," the ad proclaimed. She was named Gidget.

A phone call revealed Gidget to be a two-year-old dromedary—a one-humped camel. Gidget's owners had originally planned to breed her, but they were cutting back on their livestock operation, which included some rare species. Candy and Linda speculated on where one would find a suitable mate for a camel, especially when she was the only one in the state.

Gidget's owner was eager to find a good home for the unusual creature, and she described the camel in glowing terms. Gidget was very well behaved, accustomed to living with other livestock, and generally good-natured with other animals. "But," said her owner, "she does get jealous if too much attention is paid to the goats."

Remembering stories I'd heard about foul-tempered, spitting camels, I asked if Gidget ever showed signs of aggression. "She's not the least bit aggressive," her owner replied. In fact, the camel was at the very bottom of the pecking order among the resident cattle, sheep, and goats. "The sheep boss her around. But there are just a couple of small issues. You'll need at least a six-foot-high fence for her." Hmm, I thought. This could be a problem, since none of our haphazard fencing came anywhere near meeting that requirement.

"So you have trouble with her getting out, then?" I asked.

"No," said the woman, "Actually, Gidget hates to get out

of her pen. That's the problem. We used to have regular woven wire fencing, but we had to re-fence for Gidget. She's so tall that when she stretches her neck way over the fence to reach some particularly tasty morsel, she forgets the fence is there, and she walks right through it—she just stamps it down. When she realizes she's out of her pen, she gets upset. Then she panics. She's been injured trying to force her way back through the fence." This did not sound like the behavior of any type of livestock I had ever encountered.

"But probably the trickiest thing about Gidget," continued her owner, "is she tends to act a bit . . . giddy. When she's feeling especially happy, she gets to running and kicking up her heels. She's still young, so she's not very well coordinated. And when she starts feeling giddy, she tends to tilt her head way back, close her eyes, and just enjoy the moment as she gallops along. If a child or slow-moving animal were in her path . . . well, I really don't like to think what might happen."

Driving home from Browns Valley that afternoon, I pondered both the pros and cons of taking on Gidget, the giddy camel. On the pro side: owning a camel would be a unique experience. No one in our neighborhood had one. I conjured up grand visions of trekking down the driveway perched atop the majestic beast. Maybe I'd change her name to Jezebel or Scheherazade—something more impressive than Gidget.

On the other hand, there would be the expense and back-breaking labor of replacing miles of fencing. Not to mention the likelihood of a galloping Gidget mowing down loved ones and family pets. It was a bad idea, and I know it. But in my case, logic and common sense rarely prevailed where animals were concerned. Relegating all the negatives to the back of my mind, soon I could think only of what fun it would be to have my very own camel.

I arrived home nearly bursting with the great news. Certainly my husband would agree. We had to have Gidget.

The fleeting look of horror on Terry's face was quickly replaced by one of steely resolve. He had dealt with this type of situation before, and he knew he had to get a lid on it before it went too far.

Early in our marriage, Terry and I had assumed the roles we would play in this ongoing saga. I was the animal-loving pushover who couldn't resist the fuzzy kitten or sad-faced soon-to-be-homeless goat. Terry was forced to act as the voice of reason and practicality.

He said, "Sorry, but I really don't think we can handle a camel right now."

Terry had put his foot down. I was disappointed. I was tempted to argue with him, since I knew I could probably wear him down in time. It's been known to happen. But deep down, I knew he was right. The very last thing our menagerie needed was a giddy camel.

❋

When Terry and I were first married, we lived in an old farmhouse set on eight acres of land outside the west-central Minnesota town of Alexandria. Between us, we had two kids, two cats, and one dog. Our eight-acre parcel was big enough to provide exercise and entertainment for the pets and the children, Beth and Jon, but Terry and I weren't quite satisfied. We had both grown up on farms, and we were filled with yearning to return to an idyllic rural life—a life that may have existed only in our minds.

A few years into our marriage, we decided the time was right to expand our holdings to something that more closely resembled an actual farm, even though we would both have to keep our real jobs in town. We wanted the family farm lifestyle, and we wanted to stay in the area, but we couldn't afford to buy enough acreage and all the necessary equipment to become full-time farmers.

We met with a real estate agent to discuss the type of property we were seeking. The realtor asked Terry if he already owned farm machinery, or if he'd need to invest in that, too. When Terry described his array of aging farm equipment, the realtor said, "It sounds like you've got all the toys and you're just looking for a bigger sandbox." He had hit the nail on the head.

But as we searched for the ideal property, it became obvious that Terry's and my ideas of farming didn't much agree. When Terry thought about farming, he had visions of tractors, machinery, and cropland. For me, farming simply meant animals.

My mother always said I've been an animal lover since birth. She didn't claim this proudly. Though she never said it aloud, I'm guessing she had hoped for a daughter with clean hands and neatly combed hair, one whose clothing wasn't covered in cat hair and dog drool. Instead, she ended up with me. In childhood pictures I am always the small, scrawny figure wearing my brother's old castoff jeans, face and arms riddled with scratches, clutching a struggling kitten or puppy.

It came as no surprise to our friends and family that Terry and I ended up on eighty acres—not prime real estate by any means, but it had land to be plowed and planted, a nice flat spot for a machine shed, and plenty of space for animals.

The spinning wheel

A few years later, when my aunt Missy was cleaning out her attic as she prepared to sell her house, she discovered a spinning wheel. It was made by her great-grandfather Lars shortly after he got off the boat from Norway. Sturdy and well built, it was used by family members well into the 1940s. Since then, it had sat idle in the attic, gathering dust. According to Terry, my aunt's discovery set off the downward spiral that ended his peaceful and well-organized life.

After moving the spinning wheel downstairs, Missy started calling her nieces, beginning with the eldest, to see if a woman of the younger generation wanted this family heirloom. Two said no before she dialed my number.

I said, "Sure, I'd love to have it!" As an avid knitter, I thought it would be fun to spin my own yarn. The spinning wheel was restored to working order, and I brought it home. Once I learned to use it, the logical next step was to invest in some wool-producing livestock. Surprisingly, Terry was receptive. When he was a boy, he and his father had raised and shown sheep at county and state fairs. Terry liked to reminisce about tending the flock with his dad. I played heavily upon that sentiment, and while the rosy glow of nostalgia prevailed, Terry was persuaded to invest in a couple of sheep.

"Remember, I said *a couple* of sheep," he repeated every time the subject came up.

We spent months studying agricultural journals and sheep breeders' magazines and attending livestock shows before we decided which type of sheep we wanted to buy. Most of today's sheep have been bred specifically to produce coarse, durable wool for commercial use. Others are bred to gain lean weight rapidly and are raised as market and meat animals. Few of these modern breeds have wool that is of hand-spinning quality. We were drawn to the primitive breeds, particularly the Shetlands. Hardy and adaptable, Shetlands produce a very fine, soft fleece that is perfect for hand spinning.

Shetland sheep have evolved in relative isolation since the late eighth century. The breed originated on the Shetland Isles of Britain and is considered a primitive species, meaning humans haven't altered the breed over the centuries, aiming to create a larger animal with more meat or coarser wool. The Shetlands remain basically as they were hundreds of years ago, when they lived wild on the rocky, desolate islands off the coast of Scotland.

Shetland sheep were still rare in the United States when we bought ours in 1999. It took us a long while to find a breeder who had lambs for sale. We eventually located one in southern Minnesota, and the next day we made the four-hour drive to his farm to look at some ewe lambs.

"Two," Terry said to me again before we stepped out of the truck at the sheep farm. "We're only getting two lambs. No more than two."

"No problem," I replied. I couldn't imagine why he kept repeating that phrase.

The farmer led us to a small pen where eight ewe lambs were bunched into a corner, watching us warily. Terry inspected each lamb for general health, soundness, and conformity to breed standards. I looked to see which of the lambs had the cutest faces and the prettiest wool. Ignoring the men's sarcasm about my selection criteria, I chose two lambs. One was black, and the other was moorit—reddish brown in color.

The farmer asked, "Are you sure you want that little red one? She's a real piece of work. I can see attitude in her already." The small lamb with the determined scowl on her face was backed into a corner, head butting any other lambs that came near her.

Rather than dissuading me, the farmer's remark made the lamb seem more appealing. "We'll take her," I said before Terry could reply. I liked quirky animals. Terry didn't.

When she arrived at our farm, the little redheaded ewe looked indignantly around her as she stepped off the livestock trailer. She cast her evil eye upon every man and beast within striking distance. She made it clear right from the start that she would tolerate no intrusions on her territory.

A few weeks later, I called Terry at work. "Guess what?" I asked. For some reason Terry dislikes conversations that begin with those two words, but I was too excited to recall that fact.

"What now?" he asked.

"I just bought five more sheep."

"What?" Terry yelled into the phone. "We already have two sheep. Those two alone will produce more wool than you can spin and knit in an entire year. What on earth are we going to do with five more sheep?"

"I got a really good deal on them and just couldn't pass it up," I explained. "The only problem is we'll have to drive up to Bemidji tonight to get them."

There was silence on the other end of the line.

"Terry? Are you still there?"

"Two." He said. "Remember? You agreed we were only going to get two sheep."

"I thought you meant we could only get two *Shetland* sheep. These are Icelandic crossbreds. It's a whole different thing." Since there was no further response from Terry, I continued. "Mary was at a farm auction today," I said, referring to our friend and neighbor. "She met this couple from Bemidji who are getting out of the sheep business. They've already sold all but five of their sheep. Mary called right away to tell me about it. She didn't want us to miss out on this great deal. I called the farmer, and we can have all five ewe lambs for only two hundred dollars. I told him we'd be there tonight to pick them up."

"Remind me to thank Mary the next time I see her," Terry said before he hung up the phone.

Like their distant cousins the Shetlands, Icelandic sheep are a primitive breed. They, too, produce a fine, soft wool that is ideal for hand spinning. The crossbred lambs we bought were the offspring of a purebred Icelandic ram and ewes of other fiber breeds. Together with the Shetlands Rosie and Ada, the five Icelandic crossbreds—Gretel, Ruby, Wilson, #169, and #182—made a very handsome flock indeed.

❄

The following spring we watched our seven nubile yearling ewes frolic about the pasture, and Terry faced the inevitable next step. With remarkably little argument he agreed to the purchase of a ram. Lloyd, a registered Shetland buck, joined the family.

I was surprised when Terry agreed so easily to the idea of turning our maidenly flock into a bona fide breeding operation. But he had taken a real interest in researching the rare breeds, especially the primitive "heirloom" traits of the Shetlands, and he became even more involved when we brought home the five Icelandic crossbred ewes.

At the time we began raising them, Shetland sheep were classified as endangered by the British Rare Breeds Survival Trust, and they were at risk of extinction. Since then, they have increased in number, mainly because of their growing popularity in Canada and the United States. But in our early days of shepherding, our primitive sheep were a rarity.

Terry and I sheared the sheep manually that first year, using a hand shears that resembled a big pair of scissors or an oversized hedge trimmer. After the first shearing of our flock, we stood for a long while admiring the eight huge mounds of wool lying on a canvas tarp in the sheep shed. We were amazed at the richly colored, abundant fleeces produced by our ram and ewes. The auburn locks of Rosie, the deep ebony shades of Ada, and the varied wool of Lloyd and the Icelandic ewes—they all formed a spectrum of natural colors from a creamy white to jet black. In the following months I washed, carded, and spun each of the fleeces. Although it's a dirty, messy business, there is something truly magical in the archaic process of creating yarn wrought from dusty, smelly sheep fleeces.

From that first shearing I spun the wool and knitted dozens of pairs of mittens, socks, and hats for family and friends. I used the rest of the year's wool harvest to make braided rugs in shades of creamy white, brown, gray, and black.

By this time Terry was totally won over. The notion of helping to bring the Shetland breed back from the brink of extinction appealed to him. He also liked the utilitarian aspect of raising sheep. Unlike the countless dogs, cats, and other pets I had brought home over the years, the sheep were actually productive. And just as important to Terry, the washing, carding, and spinning of those massive fleeces kept me occupied for months at a time. I had no time to scan the pets section of the classified ads in the newspaper or drop by the local animal shelter.

Before long, Terry and I became full-fledged fiber people, traveling to conferences and shows featuring wool-producing animals and hands-on workshops ranging from ovine genetics to spinning the fleece of Himalayan yak.

That winter Terry spent nearly every evening studying reference books and manuals on primitive sheep, learning everything he could about the care and conservation of rare breeds. Over the next few years, he succumbed to the purchase of several other animals including a llama, two alpacas, two sheepdogs, and far too many angora rabbits.

My arguments in favor of these animals were always based on logic and empirical facts, and I used Terry's encyclopedic reference manuals to my best advantage. Regarding the acquisition of Camilla the llama: "Terry, did you know llamas are often used as guardians of sheep, keeping away stray dogs and coyotes? I read all about it in your book about the preservation of heritage breeds."

Dogs: "Terry, your *Encyclopedia of Sheep* says that we need special herding dogs if we're going to have any luck controlling these wild, primitive breeds of sheep."

Rabbits: "Look here, this chapter of *Exotic Animals for Fun and Profit* says sheep's wool can be blended with angora rabbit's wool to make a special kind of yarn. Just *look* at those cute bunnies in the picture!"

To each of these suggestions, Terry's first response was "*No!* Absolutely no more animals!" Each time, after weeks of listening to my persuasive appeals, he began to wear down. By the third week of negotiations Terry's answer became a cautious, "We'll see." By week four, he had usually weakened sufficiently. His final weary reply was, "I'll get the truck."

In this way, our diverse flock has grown with each passing year. In addition to the llamas, alpacas, rabbits, cats, and dogs, we have built up a flock of thirty Shetland and Icelandic sheep, each with a beautiful fleece and a distinct personality.

Something's got to give

When we bought our first sheep in 1999, Terry and I both worked at full-time jobs in town. I was a grant writer for a nonprofit agency, and Terry worked as a metrology technician—a specialist in the calibration of precision measuring instruments—at 3M's Alexandria plant.

In some ways, we were an unlikely couple. While in high school and college, I had suffered through endless courses in algebra, calculus, and physics. I often complained, "What's the point? Who ever uses this stuff in real life?" My college major was art, and my friends teased me about my aversion to math and science courses. No one would have guessed I was destined to marry the only person I'd ever meet who actually uses the mathematical ratio pi in his daily work.

But one thing Terry and I had in common was the sheep. We found that the daily care and feeding wasn't too hard to fit into our schedules, even with our full-time day jobs. But the seasonal activities such as haying, shearing, and harvesting caused more of a strain when combined with our off-farm work. The old adage says, "Make hay while the sun shines." The weather in Minnesota is unpredictable, and when the hay crop is ready to be cut and baled or the grain is ready for harvest, those tasks take absolute priority for full-time farmers.

When both the farmer and his wife work in town, most of the critical daylight hours are lost. There is nothing more frustrating for the part-time farmer than waking up to a clear, sunny day, knowing he's got acres of hay cut and ready to bale—but having to turn his back on the crop and head off into town for work.

Though we weren't unhappy with our jobs, the lure of staying home to cultivate crops and animals was hard to resist. As our multi-species flock grew, so did our desire to escape our nine-to-five office jobs. Terry dreamed of being able to farm full-time, spending his days planting and harvesting crops and tending to the sheep. I longed to be able to supervise full-time the annual cycle of lambing, shearing, grazing, and breeding that was consuming more and more of our attention. And I really wanted to devote more time to spinning and fiber arts.

At about this same time, Terry and I realized that we may have taken on more than we could handle. The basic farm chores were manageable, and even the extra seasonal projects weren't a deal breaker. It was the wool processing that was really wearing us out.

After we sheared the animals in the spring, the shorn fleeces were stored in a loft in the machine shed. Before the wool could be spun, I had to sort, trim, and repeatedly hand-wash each of the fleeces in old-fashioned washtubs set up in the back yard. After washing, I laid the heavy, wet fleeces on raised screens to air dry. The next step was hand carding and ultimately spinning the wool into yarn. Each of these steps was remarkably time-consuming and labor-intensive.

To make matters worse, our supply of unlimited free labor

was running out. By this time, both Beth and Jon had finished high school and left home. Christopher, born shortly after the move, was only seven years old when we bought the sheep, and even Terry had to agree that he was too young for much manual labor.

It seemed that we spent all of our free time trying to meet the growing demand for hand-spun yarn and wool products. We were also getting more and more requests to do wool carding and spinning demonstrations at fairs and festivals. Individuals and groups of crafters asked to tour our farm to get a closer look at the rare Shetland sheep and other fiber-bearing animals.

What began as a pleasant diversion had slowly and in-sidiously transformed into a demanding full-time commit-ment. The heritage sheep and fiber projects had become too extensive and time-consuming to be considered hobbies any longer.

One particularly grueling fall day, about five years after we bought our first sheep, matters came to a head. Both Terry and I had put in a full day's work at our regular jobs. We rushed home, changed clothes, and raced outside to start the chores. We didn't finish until almost ten o'clock, when we returned to the house, nearly collapsing with exhaustion. This type of schedule was becoming more and more common. It was then we finally faced up to the fact that something had to change. We couldn't continue at this pace.

"It's not fair to us, or to Chris," said Terry. "All we do is work. We haven't taken a real vacation in years."

I thought wistfully of the family vacations we enjoyed be-fore we bought the sheep. There were leisurely road trips to both coasts and a couple of excursions to Europe. During the first fifteen years of our marriage, we had hiked, biked, and dragged apathetic teenagers to see the Grand Canyon and nearly all of the other natural wonders America had to offer.

But since we began raising sheep, we had only taken a few long weekends away from the farm.

Over the next days we had some serious discussions about how to resolve our situation. Though it sometimes felt like the sheep and wool projects had completely taken over our lives, we weren't ready to abandon them just yet.

We agreed. Something had to give. If we weren't willing to quit the sheep and wool processing activities, one of us would need to give up his or her job in town to stay home and man-age the farm. Terry was the logical candidate for this position, since much of the work involved heavy lifting and other stren-uous tasks, but there were two complications. Terry held the highest-paying job, and his employer provided the family's health insurance.

It was a no-brainer. I would quit my job to stay at home and become a full-time shepherdess and wool spinner. "Yippee!" I shouted when the decision was finalized. I was ecstatic.

Shepherdess

Right from the start I knew the life of a shepherdess would not be easy. Money would be tight and the work would be hard. I would spend very little time lounging serenely on a grassy hillside, watching over the sheep as they grazed pastorally in the distance. But at the same time, I knew the work would be satisfying. And since I'd be handling most of the farm chores during the day, my family would have more free time in the evenings and on weekends.

When Chris had friends over to visit, I was always surprised at how little most of them knew about what their parents did for a living. Parents got up in the morning, went off to work, and returned home in the evening. The children accepted this as normal procedure and didn't seem too curious about what their parents were up to all day long.

Growing up on a farm, my brother and I knew all too well what our parents were up to, because we were usually required to participate in whatever activity was under way. We drove tractors, baled hay, chased cattle, and when evening came, we mowed the lawn for entertainment. When there were no crops to harvest or livestock to tend, we touched up the paint on the outbuildings to keep ourselves out of mischief. Strange as it may seem, I couldn't have asked for a better life. I wanted to replicate that feeling of family unity and involvement with my own children. Two of them had already escaped, but I still had a chance with Chris.

Within a week of beginning my new career as head shepherdess, a regular routine developed. By seven o'clock in the morning Christopher was safely aboard the school bus, and my work day began. I washed and rinsed the breakfast dishes, stacked them in the drainer, then headed outside to check on the animals. Though no snow had fallen, already the ground was iron-hard and covered by a thick white rime. The stiff, frosty grass crunched under my boots as I strode across the yard.

My first stop each morning was the kennel, where enthusiastic yips and leaps and lolling tongues showed the dogs' eagerness to start their day. Two of them, Bart and Petey, were Shetland sheepdogs in the early stages of training. Our daughter Beth's pets, Keeyla and Karsey, were temporarily staying with us. Though their visit had already lasted more than two years, Terry still insisted we weren't going to keep them permanently.

Once the dogs were set free and their mad dash around the farm had begun, I let the sheep out of their shed and into the pasture. Though the grass was brown and withered, the sheep still enjoyed the token ritual of grazing, and they spent most of their day outdoors.

Like the dogs, the sheep were always champing at the bit to escape the confines of the shed and run free. When I opened the gate leading from the shed to the pasture, the sheep burst through the small opening in a huge, woolen explosion. As one, the entire shifting mass of galloping fleece, heads, and hooves thundered through the narrow gate and disappeared over the hill.

When the sheep had been out of their shed for about an hour, I hiked out to check on them. By that time they would have worked their way to the farthest end of the pasture. This early morning jaunt was and remains one of my favorite parts of the day.

The main pasture extends alongside our half-mile gravel driveway. The pasture is made up of three smaller enclosures, one or two of which are often closed off to allow for rotational grazing. But in late fall, the gates to each of the three enclosures were open, and the sheep could wander as far as a half mile from home.

While writing a grant proposal for a flood diversion project, I had recently learned a new expression: *uneconomic remnant*. In civil engineering terms, that phrase is used to describe a scrap of land that is left stranded when property is acquired or taken by eminent domain for a construction project. The uneconomic remnant is typically inaccessible by road, and because of its isolated nature, it has little monetary value or productive use. The term struck a chord with me, and I realized that—except for the winding dirt road connecting us to the county highway—our farm fit that description perfectly.

Our land was not much good for growing crops. The tillable acreage was bisected by too many hills, too much water, and too many trees to be considered prime agricultural land. The steep hills were a constant hazard for tractor and implement navigation. One had to be ever vigilant to prevent a rollover on the side hills when baling hay. Just about the only thing our land was good for was pasturing sheep.

Lake Mina lies along the eastern border of our farm. It is not the type of lake where tourists like to vacation. Lake Mina has no sandy public beaches. Instead it has a muddy bottom with cattail reeds lining the shore, deep unfathomable drop-offs, mysterious sunken islands, and an occasional floating bog. Despite these hazards, it is a great spot for fishing and an even better place to row out upon on a still summer evening. Only two other houses are visible across the lake, and most of the shoreline consists of green pastures, fields, and woods.

Our uneconomic remnant may not be a valuable piece of farmland, but it is a restful and pleasant place to live. I never tire of looking over our small kingdom with its variety of aspect and landscape.

One of the best views unfolds in the morning as I pass through the last of the three gates leading to the farthest pasture. The scene is magical on a cool, damp morning, when the pasture is shrouded in mist and fog rising off the adjacent lake. The sheep tend to congregate in a certain low, marshy spot, where the grass grows thick and lush. They are hidden beneath a heavy blanket of low-lying fog, but I can hear their muted *baa*s and the disembodied jangling of Rosie's bell. Off in the distance, where the invisible flock is grazing, Tony the alpaca's head and long, bobbing neck emerge from the swirling mist. It's eerie, like the dawning of the day in some prehistoric meadow, with Tony portraying a dinosaur—or perhaps the Loch Ness monster—rising out of the murky primordial vapors.

After checking to see that everyone is present and accounted for, I walk back to the farmyard and continue with the day's business. At that time of year, my midmorning work usually involves manhandling hay bales and mixing the day's ration of the rabbits' special blend of feed. Later, when winter arrives in all its blustery, frigid glory, the morning chores include battling frozen pipes and carrying endless buckets of water to the livestock.

The coats of the angora rabbits grow thick and vibrant during the coldest months of the year. Their winter colors are bright and vivid—as clear and striking as the jagged ice crystals forming on the surface of the sheep's water trough. In the summer months, the rabbits' coats grow less enthusiastically, and they take on more muted, almost pastel, shades. Winter's hardships bring out the brilliance in everything on the farm. A good dose of suffering is regarded as a constructive thing among the old-timers in this Norwegian Lutheran community. We were all raised to believe that no good comes from anything that is attained too easily.

By noon the first round of outdoor activities is complete. With rosy cheeks and tingling fingers and toes, I reach my daily quota of suffering outside in the cold, and I return to the warmth of the house to start my wool work.

When I'm seated at the old spinning wheel, the afternoon hours seem to fly by, as the wheel and I work in tandem to craft soft, earth-toned yarns. It doesn't matter whether the wool I'm spinning is from angora rabbits, alpacas, llamas, or sheep. The process of spinning is rhythmic, timeless, and utterly absorbing. It becomes an almost hypnotic progression, from guiding raw fiber into the small orifice of the whirling apparatus to watching it evolve and emerge as richly colored strands building up on the bobbin. Handfuls of angora rabbit's wool, or the more deeply colored alpaca or sheep's wool, seem to melt in my hands as the spinning wheel steadily pulls and twists the fiber into a thin, single strand of yarn. The single strands of yarn are then plied together, three at a time, to create skein after skein of naturally hued yarns.

On winter evenings Terry, Chris, and I relaxed together in our small living room. Terry, stretched out in his recliner, studied his sheep manuals, Chris did homework or played games on the computer, and I knit. I knit the hand-spun yarn into many different things, but mostly I made mittens.

A regional newspaper ran a feature article on our rabbits' wool mittens. The article praised the virtues of rabbit's wool, describing its luxurious warmth (rabbit's wool is seven times warmer than sheep's wool), its downy softness, and light-as-a-feather qualities. The article was published in early December, and by Christmas I had almost fifty orders for mittens. I knitted industriously all winter long.

Though business was booming, it was not a lucrative undertaking. I charged thirty to forty dollars for a pair of hand-spun, hand-knit mittens. Some prospective buyers were shocked at the price: "But I can buy a pair of mittens at Wal Mart for five dollars!"

One of the drawbacks of the home-spun woolen business is that every step of the process is prohibitively time-consuming. Once wool is shorn from the animal, it must be repeatedly washed and then carded before spinning. It takes hours to spin enough wool for a pair of mittens, and it takes at least five more hours to knit the mittens. Even at forty dollars a pair, I was making less than five dollars an hour for the spinning and knitting. And that did not take into consideration the value of the wool itself, or the time spent shearing, washing, and carding. Not to mention the feeding and care of the livestock who produced the wool. All told, we once calculated that we earned about fifty cents an hour on hand-spun, hand-knit items.

I sometimes sold the wool, yarn, and knitted items at craft and fiber shows. People continued to seek us out, asking to see the fiber-bearing animals and to see firsthand how wool was carded and spun.

❋

That winter was a serene and heavenly time. The sheep were settled and quiet, awaiting the birth of their lambs. Other than feeding and watering, the flock needed little attention during those coldest months of the year.

I loved the freedom winter gave me to spend hours working with the fiber—spinning, designing, and knitting. In spring, summer, and fall, there are so many important jobs to be done outside, and the farmer or shepherd spends much of the day outdoors, no matter what the weather brings. But in December and January, I felt very little guilt at staying inside. I caught up on the knitting orders and even built up a small inventory of finished mittens.

After those cold months, February started out warm and balmy. With several days of above-freezing temperatures early in the month, everyone began to look forward to spring. Emerging from their winter quasi-hibernation state, the sheep slowly came back to life as the weather warmed. In their advanced stages of pregnancy, the ewes became irritable and balky. Head butting, feet stamping, and angry *baa*s resonated through the sheep shed.

In preparation for lambing, Terry set up some small pens in the sheep shed. These lambing pens enclose a ewe and her newborn lamb in a small space, encouraging them to become acquainted and protecting the newborn from being trampled by the rest of the flock. They would also let us watch the lambs more closely in those critical first hours. Over the next two months, the lambing pens would be taken down, moved, set up again, and rearranged as needed. Sometimes six or more pens were occupied by ewes and their new lambs.

But for now, the pens were empty, and anticipation hung in the air. I spent a lot of time simply standing and admiring the hugely pregnant ewes, and I was reminded of the feeling I had as a child gazing at the pile of brightly wrapped presents waiting under the tree on Christmas Eve.

Finally, the weather broke, and the lambs began to arrive.

Lamb Chop

That February day dawned sunny but cold, with a brisk biting wind that made my eyes water as I crossed the yard to the sheep shed. The ewes were entrenched in the warm shed, munching hay, either nursing newborn lambs or waiting with ponderous bellies. It was lambing season, the time of year when—after five months of relative peace and quiet—utter chaos erupts in the ovine world.

In spring, the sheep shed is filled with excitement, drama, and stress. It's like a busy hospital maternity ward with a bunch of uncooperative, highly excitable, non-English-speaking women going into labor all at once. Our maternity ward was staffed by an individual with no medical training (me), and at the best of times by two people, one of whom had just finished a long day's work in town (Terry). A third reinforcement (Chris) could be called upon in times of dire emergency if he could be torn away from the video game controller that seemed to have permanently taken root in his hand.

During that time of year, we checked often for new lambs

or signs of sheep that were about to deliver. Terry checked the sheep early in the morning before he left for work, and I checked them several times throughout the day.

The ewes gathered around the hayrack expectantly when I entered the shed. I tossed a few forkfuls of hay into the feeders and looked closely over the shed's occupants. Some of the older ewes had given birth in the previous days. These were experienced mothers, and they had borne this year's crop of lambs with no need of intervention.

Off in a corner, one ewe nervously guarded a wobbly newborn lamb. She stamped her foot when any of the other sheep came near her, and she glared at me as I came toward her. I reached down to pet and reassure Ruby, the new mother. When she was comfortable with my presence, I examined her tiny black lamb, still wet and struggling to get to its feet. The lamb looked healthy and strong. Carrying him in the crook of my elbow, I used him as bait to lure his mother into the nearest empty lambing pen.

While spreading straw in the pen and hanging a heat lamp for the new arrival, I heard a muffled sound from the haystack on the far side of the building. It sounded like some kind of animal cry, but I couldn't tell what kind. Was it a rabid raccoon, or maybe an injured stray cat hiding in the haystack? The sheep heard the distressed cries, too, and the entire flock stopped noshing long enough to fix their shepherd with an expectant group stare.

"Don't look at me!" I scolded. It was apparent they expected me to investigate and handle whatever crisis had arisen within the haystack. I continued to fiddle with the heat lamp, ignoring for the moment the muffled howls and the thirty pairs of eyes boring into my back. When the newborn lamb was laid on the straw beneath the illuminated heat lamp, Ruby eagerly followed her new baby into the enclosure. She made an affectionate chuckling sound deep in her throat and the lamb responded with a tiny *baaaa*. The ewe nuzzled her baby as he weaved his way through the knee-deep straw toward her udder.

Rewarding as it was to watch the interaction between mother and baby, curiosity got the best of me, and I turned to investigate the strange sound in the haystack. To more easily trace the desperate cries, I shooed all of the sheep, except for those in lambing pens, out of the shed. Armed with an old broom handle for self-defense, I examined the eight-foot pile of hay bales. It was evident the enraged creature was either hiding or trapped somewhere very deep inside. I removed the bales one by one from the towering stack, all the while praying for deliverance from the angry spirit soon to be released. I continued moving bales until the sound was quite clear, and I knew I was getting close to the source. In one hand I held my whacking stick, ready to confront whatever lay in wait.

Finally, sweating and exhausted, I lifted a bale near the base of the stack. Something moved stealthily into the dark space between two bales on the very bottom row. I jumped back, whacking stick at the ready, and prepared to do battle.

A fuzzy white head popped up from the crack. It was a newborn lamb. She shook her tiny white head vigorously, releasing a cloud of alfalfa particles and dust. The lamb looked around curiously and bleated as if to say, "It's about time you got me out of there!"

The rabid, foaming-at-the-mouth animal I'd envisioned had suddenly morphed into a tiny, fuzzy ewe lamb. I set aside my whacking stick, relieved that none of the sheep were present to witness my humiliation. I scooped the little creature into my arms and brought her into the rectangle of weak wintry sunlight that filtered through the open shed door.

From the look of it, the lamb had been born sometime during the previous night. She must have wandered away from the other sheep and crawled under the board fence and into the haystack. She squeezed into a narrow space between the bales and kept moving forward until she reached a dead end. She couldn't turn around, and she didn't have the sense to back out.

Despite the traumatic adventure, the lamb seemed healthy and sound. Not your typical weak and wobbly baby, this one was feisty and loud. Her incessant bellowing demanded that someone produce milk for her immediately.

The lamb had been cleaned up and obviously cared for by its mother in the hour after its birth. Mother and baby would have had plenty of opportunity to bond during the time it took the ewe to lick the lamb clean and dry. Without the diligent and immediate attention of its mother, a newborn lamb will usually die before taking its first steps. We had seen instances of that with first-time mothers who failed to rip the amniotic sac from their lambs' faces. When that happened, we found the newly born lamb dead, still enclosed in a placenta shroud, while its mother stood nearby bleating sadly.

Clearly, that was not the situation with this lamb. Never before had I met a newborn with such vigor and such a well-developed set of lungs. "Okay," I told her as I tucked her under my arm, "We'll go find your mother right away. I bet she'll be glad to see you."

Certain that the mother would claim her baby once the two were reunited, I carried the bawling lamb out to the pasture. We neared the area where the sheep were gathered, and each ewe lifted her head in alarm. The entire flock then dispersed abruptly, galloping off to the far corners of the pasture. They reacted as if I were carrying a ticking time bomb instead of a newborn lamb. All the while, the lamb was churning its legs and wailing like a mad cat.

I had a pretty good idea of who the negligent mother was. Using the process of elimination, I was able to pare down the list of likely suspects quite rapidly. At the top of the list was

Gretel, a small brown ewe who—up until yesterday—had been sluggish and heavily burdened by her ever-expanding pregnant girth.

Narrowing my eyes against the cold wind, I watched Gretel streak across the pasture in her new, svelte body. She must have given birth during the night, but no baby ran by her side.

I spent the next hour trying to corner and capture Gretel. Normally, the sight and sound of her lamb will ignite a spark of recognition within a ewe. But Gretel—more than any of the other sheep—appeared to be terrified of the bleating bundle in my arms.

Neither chasing, nor yelling, nor luring with a bucket of grain succeeded in bringing the wary ewe into the shed, where I hoped to pen her in with the new lamb. Certainly she would accept the baby if only the two could be confined in a small space and left alone together.

After more than an hour of frustrating and exhausting pursuit, I gave up on capturing the elusive Gretel. I retreated to the house with the complaining lamb still tucked under one arm. I set the lamb in a cardboard box in the kitchen while I called the vet clinic to ask for suggestions. Shetland sheep are instinctively good mothers, usually requiring little help at lambing time. In four years, this was our first abandoned lamb.

The veterinarian who answered the phone was familiar with our collection of cats, dogs, and assorted other pets. I explained this was my first experience caring for an abandoned lamb and asked for his advice. It was hard to carry on a conversation over the din of the squalling lamb.

The vet said, "These first hours are critical. The lamb needs to have colostrum, the first milk that the ewe produces after a birth. I hate to say it, but that lamb's probably not going to survive without the protein and antibodies in the colostrum."

Straining to hear him, I moved into the living room, stretching the phone cord to its limit. By now the house cats had been alerted to the presence of an intruder. Mr. and Mrs. Tinkles stood at my feet, staring up at me as if demanding an explanation for this unspeakable turn of events. They flicked their tails in anger while darting annoyed glances first at me and then at the cardboard box harboring the unwelcome guest. Their naps had been interrupted, their space was invaded, and they wanted that noisy thing out of the house immediately.

The vet continued. "I'd recommend that you go back out and catch the mother. Milk her, and then bottle-feed her milk to the lamb. We've got bottles and nipples here at the clinic."

The vet's advice sounded good in theory, and it probably would have worked fine if Gretel were a placid old cow. But she bore more resemblance to a crafty mountain goat, and I doubted that either the lamb or I could get anywhere near her udder. Unwilling to face yet another marathon session with Gretel, I decided to seek a second opinion.

I picked up the phone again and dialed the number of my friend Luan. Luan is a female jack-of-all-trades whose life and career paths have taken many a turn. People often remark on Luan's uncanny resemblance to a Barbie doll. With her petite figure, blond good looks, classy wardrobe, and vivacious personality, it's easy to see the similarity. But beneath that glamorous exterior lurks a tough woman who has overcome much adversity. Luan has faced situations that would send Barbie scampering back to her dream house in horror, never to emerge again.

When Luan found herself at loose ends after a divorce, she wasted no time in starting over. She embraced her new life with enthusiasm, moving to a new community and landing three part-time jobs. In a burst of energy, Luan bought an old house in need of repair. She was doing the bulk of the renovations herself. It was exhausting work, but Luan is capable of just about anything.

Luan is a fount of information on the care and nurturing of all kinds of livestock. When she was married, she managed a large dairy herd. Luan handled huge Holstein dairy cows and did most of the milking and farm chores, while bearing and raising four children in her spare time. She was kicked by cows, mauled by bulls, and nearly squashed to death between an angry Holstein and a barn wall. Through all of this, Luan has always been positive and enthusiastic; she has the best outlook on life of anyone I know.

Luan was staffing a newly opened mortgage company, and she usually had time to talk. The company was still in its start-up phase, and business wasn't too brisk.

"Hello, this is Luan," she answered cheerfully on the first ring. When she recognized it was me at the other end of the line, her tone changed dramatically. "Oh. It's you."

"Well, thanks," I said. "It's good to hear your voice, too."

"This isn't about adopting another animal, is it?" Luan had become a bit leery of my generosity lately. A few years earlier, I had given her a rabbit. Stella was a beloved pet, named after Luan's great-aunt, but she had proved to be a high-maintenance responsibility during the upheaval in Luan's life. Now the real issue was Tux, the dog. Despite the mixed success with Stella, I had recently arranged for Luan to adopt the small black terrier.

"How's Tux doing?" I asked.

"He's about the same," she sighed. "I'm just afraid one of these days he'll jump right out of his skin, he's so high-strung. Last night I left him alone in the yard for about ten minutes and he nearly scratched all the paint off the front door trying to get back in."

"Well, all I need today is some advice," I reassured Luan. "I don't have any animals to give away at the moment."

"Thank God for that!" she said. "What's the problem?"

I explained to her my predicament with the abandoned

newborn and the evasive Gretel. I asked if anywhere in her vast experience with livestock, she had run into something similar.

"I've never raised sheep myself, but I do remember something my neighbor Axel used to say," Luan continued. "He always said that the best way to deal with a situation where a ewe doesn't accept her newborn lamb is to simulate a birth."

Luan went on to describe old Axel's gruesome procedure, which involved restraining the ewe, then inserting one's hand into her uterus. The hand is formed into a fist, then slowly pulled out of the ewe's womb. The resulting sensation makes the ewe feel as though she has just given birth. She turns around looking for the lamb she believes she has produced. At that point the unwanted lamb is shoved under the ewe's nose with the hope that she will accept it the second time around.

When she finished her graphic step-by-step description of the procedure, I thought about it for a moment, then said, "I don't think I'm quite desperate enough to try that yet."

"Suit yourself," said Luan as she hung up the phone.

※

I pulled on my boots and headed back outside. After checking the shed for new lambs, I made one last attempt to catch Gretel. Once again she proved elusive. By now she had figured out my game plan, and she wanted none of it. She had forgotten all about giving birth, and she was determined not to be saddled with the loud squawking object that I kept trying to foist on her. Besides, having rested from her earlier exertions, she was looking forward to another round of racing wildly around the pasture. I was not.

It's often said that sheep are stupid creatures, but I know they have enough smarts to take a particular delight in getting the best of their shepherds. And they get the best of us all too often, which makes me think that they are not as stupid as they would have us believe.

When Terry and Chris returned home that afternoon, we spent another hour trying to apprehend Gretel. Finally, when it seemed that we would never catch her, she made a tactical error while cornered in the small yard just outside the shed. Gretel hesitated one second too long before dashing away, and Terry managed to grab hold of her heavy fleece. He guided her into a lambing pen in the sheep shed.

Since Gretel had proved to be such an escape artist, Terry found a hammer and a handful of nails, adding another foot of board fence to the top of the pen. "There's no way she'll get out of that pen now," Terry said. He removed his cap and wiped the sweat from his brow. "And if she does get out, she's a free woman. I'm not going after her again."

Chris carried the loud, hungry lamb from the house and set her in the pen with Gretel. The lamb immediately went to work at obtaining her long-awaited meal. But the moment the lamb latched onto a nipple, Gretel reacted with a swift kick that sent her baby flying in a high arc across the pen. The lamb hit the far wall with a thud and landed in a heap on the floor.

Chris ran to the lamb to see if it had been injured. Undaunted, the little lamb struggled to her feet, shook herself off, and approached her wary mother again. Terry grabbed Gretel's head and held her still so the baby could nurse.

When the feeding was over, we took the lamb out of the pen for her own safety. Gretel made it clear that though she might tolerate this outrageous intrusion on her udder while she was restrained, she wouldn't treat the lamb kindly if she were left alone with it.

With a bit of warm milk in her stomach the lamb became a totally different creature. The noisy, desperate cries stopped. The lamb seemed unfazed by her mother's abusive treatment. She scampered playfully across the shed, looking over her shoulder and daring Chris to follow her. She glowed with contentment, curiosity, and good cheer. It was amazing how the tiny lamb bounced back after each of the hard knocks she had taken in her short life. Before she was even a day old, the lamb's distinctive personality began to blossom.

Chris and I wanted to keep the lamb in the house for a week or two, bottle-feeding and making a pet of her. But Terry—always the voice of reason—stressed the importance of the mother's milk and the nutrients and antibodies it contained. "You wouldn't be doing her a favor by making a bottle lamb out of her," he said. "She'll be far better off in the long run if she's raised on her mother's milk and kept in the shed with the other sheep."

I had to appreciate his point. Terry respects the heritage breed characteristics and works hard to preserve them. In their natural environment, the primitive breeds of sheep live hardy and independent lives. Terry does his best to replicate the natural diet and habitat of the Shetland and Icelandic sheep. And, as much as possible, we avoid the dosing, drenching, injecting, and docking that are usually associated with sheep production. While commercial flocks are fed grain supplements to encourage multiple births and a meatier product for slaughter, our sheep thrive on a diet consisting primarily of pasture grass and hay with minimal alfalfa content. Rather than relying on chemical herbicides and pesticides, we practice pasture rotation and other organic methods to control parasites and weeds. As a result, the flock has been healthy. Our lean ewes have little trouble with lambing, compared with fattened grain-fed sheep. And we believe that the limited use of chemicals is a positive thing for all of us.

We do few of the things commercial breeders do to increase profits, and though our farming operation is often financially strapped, the sheep enjoy an existence befitting their heritage. Terry also believes in allowing the sheep to live as independently as possible—with little human intervention—much as they would in their natural island environment. This particular theory of Terry's is in constant conflict with my subversive efforts to make pets out of the lambs.

Terry and I reached a compromise on how the lamb should be raised. We continued to confine the obstinate Gretel and force her to feed her baby twice each day, and we supplemented those feedings with milk replacer from a bottle.

This plan worked well for the first two days. But by the third day of Gretel's confinement, she'd had enough. When Terry approached with the lamb tucked under his arm for the evening feeding, Gretel backed into a corner, hunkered down, and made one almighty leap that carried her over the top of the high-sided lambing pen and out the partially open shed door. We caught a fleeting glimpse of her wooly backside vanishing into the darkness, and then she was gone.

Terry and I stood in stunned silence for a moment. Neither of us had ever seen a sheep make such a jump. It was impossible. When the shock wore off, Terry dropped the struggling lamb into my arms. "Looks like you got yourself a bottle lamb," he said with a grin.

I carried the lamb back to the house and warmed a bottle for her. Anticipating months of pampering and spoiling the tiny creature, I hoped she had received enough of the life-saving colostrum to bolster her immune system. Though she would have to settle for a food that was less nutritionally ideal than her mother's milk, she would be more than compensated by the love and attention showered upon her.

Gretel's abandoned lamb quickly became a family pet. Chris named her Lamb Chop after a puppet he played with as a baby. She did resemble the soft fluffy character with the long eyelashes, but she proved to be far more robust than her lifeless cotton namesake.

Tux

B efore Luan adopted Tux, he belonged to my future son-in-law, Jeremy. When he was in college, Jeremy had acquired Tux from an animal shelter. The small black terrier had white chest markings that resembled a tuxedo. After wreaking havoc in the lives of a string of unfortunate owners, Tux had found himself—yet again—on death row at the dog pound. Due to the frequency and nature of his past indiscretions, it was unlikely there would be a last-minute call from the governor granting a reprieve for Tux. Jeremy happened to be at the animal shelter just hours before Tux was scheduled to be put to sleep. Being a compassionate soul, Jeremy adopted the lively little terrier and brought him home.

The bachelor life agreed with Tux. He lived happily with Jeremy and his roommates in a big house in Minneapolis. Things went well for Jeremy and Tux until Jeremy became en- gaged to my daughter, Beth. By this time Tux was nearly nine years old, sporting a gray muzzle and potbelly.

When Beth first met Tux, she felt sorry for the old dog. Jeremy had told her about Tux's checkered past and multiple stays at various animal shelters. Beth wondered why Tux had had such bad luck with his previous owners. It didn't take long for her to find out. Once she got to know him, she realized Tux was like nothing she had ever seen before. A whirling dervish. A Tasmanian devil. An absolute madman.

Even at his advanced age, Tux was so full of nervous energy that he was never still—not even in his sleep. He was constantly running, twitching, leaping, whining, and barking. Anyone who showed him even a bit of attention was nearly knocked over by the overexcited dog.

Tux literally bounced off the walls, off the furniture, and over the sofa. He ran through the house, racing from kitchen to living room to dining room and then back again. This pattern was repeated over and over daily. To top it all off, Tux suffered a lethal gas problem: his toxic emissions could clear a room in seconds.

When Jeremy and his roommates had company, Tux shifted his performance into high gear. One of Tux's favorite party tricks was to gallop up from behind the sofa, then leap over its back, landing in the laps of the unsuspecting guests. Luckily for Tux, Jeremy and his bachelor friends were easygoing and tolerant.

Then Beth and Jeremy got engaged. As the date of the wedding approached, Beth's nerves began to frazzle. Tux's antics were annoying at the best of times, but added to the stress of the upcoming wedding, Tux and his offensive stunts became almost unbearable.

One day Beth arrived at Jeremy's with a stack of wedding invitations to be addressed. Jeremy was not at home, but Tux was. Beth set the invitations on the kitchen table and gave Tux a scowl that sent him scurrying from the room.

Since Jeremy was out, Beth took the opportunity to try on

the wedding dress she had just picked up at the bridal shop. She brought in the long white gown from her car, lifted the dress out of its box, and carefully arranged it over the couch, lovingly smoothing out the creases.

Meanwhile, Tux knew he needed to redeem himself with his master's soon-to-be wife. He crept back into the room, hoping to gain some positive attention from his future mistress. In his nervousness, he suffered a particularly nasty gas attack, which sent Beth reeling. Sensing he had captured her attention, Tux decided to seize the moment and really show her what he could do. After making a few fast and frenetic circles through the house, he made one final victory lap and launched himself over the back of the couch with unbridled enthusiasm. It was one of his best performances, and he was proud of himself.

*

That evening I got a phone call from Beth. The call began quite normally with an update on the wedding preparations, but I could tell she had something else on her mind.

Finally, the real purpose of Beth's phone call came out. "Do you want another dog?" she asked. There was more than a hint of desperation in her voice. "Jeremy's dog Tux is a really nice dog but I just don't know if I want a dog right now and I think it would be nice if he could live out in the country where there's room to run and play with the other dogs and . . ."

I cut her off in mid-sentence. "Oh, no. I don't think so. Not this time. Just yesterday Terry said we have way too many dogs here already. He says four dogs are at least three too many." I reminded her that we were still boarding the two dogs she left with us when she moved from a house to an apartment in Minneapolis.

"Well, would you just see if you can find someone who

wants a dog?" I could hear Beth was nearly in tears over the matter. I assured her I would see what I could do.

-❈-

A few days later I was having lunch with Luan. We usually met for lunch every week or two, but lately our get-togethers had become less frequent. With her three jobs and home renovation project, we were lucky to see each other once a month. Though she was happy with her new life she said, "What I really miss from those days on the farm are the animals. I'd like to have a dog, but I'm just so busy with everything else right now."

Immediately I thought of Tux. Wouldn't this be a match made in heaven? A dog needing a home and a woman needing a dog. Luan was patient and kind, and I suspected Tux would need an owner with both of those characteristics. I told Luan about Tux's plight and asked her to think about it.

Meanwhile, Beth was e-mailing me daily dispatches describing Tux and his wonderful attributes. She asked me to forward these messages to Luan, hoping to sway her decision. Beth sent photos of Tux's sad face with the long gray muzzle. Her descriptions of Tux were accurate, but vague. "Energetic. Loves people. Enjoys exercise. Likes to play. Doesn't eat much." There was no mention of the frantic episodes of running and couch-leaping. Nor the vomiting or gas attacks.

Finally Luan caved in and agreed to take the dog. After a brief settling-in period, Luan and Tux seemed to be getting along well. Her need to nurture and his need for attention meshed perfectly. During their first days together, Luan gave glowing reports of the little dog's exemplary behavior. But I couldn't shake the uneasy feeling that Tux was simply biding his time, knowing he needed to get a toehold on Luan's affections before he could allow his true personality to emerge. I was certain the old dog still had more tricks up his sleeve.

Whiplash

By the first of March, the newborn Lamb Chop was thriving on her bottle-fed diet. Just as Terry predicted, she had become an attention-seeking, underfoot pest. She missed no opportunity to beg for bottles and cry for attention. She bore no resemblance to her proud and independent island-dwelling ancestors, and she had absolutely no time for other sheep.

Lamb Chop loved her bottle, and she was often a little too enthusiastic at feeding time. Like a badly behaved dog, she jumped up onto the person holding the bottle, leaving muddy hoofprints everywhere. She tagged along behind Chris and me as we did our chores around the farm. Lamb Chop became the pet of the family that summer, but by the time she was three weeks old, Lamb Chop had a rival for her bottle.

Though she was never blessed with a proper name, #169 was one of my favorite ewes. Her wool was actually black in color, but #169's fleece faded in the summer sun to a deep reddish brown. This fleece spun up into a soft, gorgeous auburn yarn. Not only did she have a lovely fleece, #169 also had a strong mothering instinct. She had already produced six healthy lambs for us, and she always took meticulous care of her babies.

A few weeks after Lamb Chop was born, #169 delivered a single dark brown lamb during the night. Neither Terry nor I was present for the delivery, but it appeared to have been a routine birth. All seemed to be well with mother and baby, although #169 seemed a bit listless.

But by the next day, we knew something was wrong: #169 was distressed, refusing to eat. The vet had come to do some other work on our farm, and we asked him to take a look at her.

When Dan had finished examining #169, he turned to face Terry and me. "I'm afraid she's got another lamb still inside her." He shook his head grimly. "The lamb's dead, and it feels like a big one. It's an awkward presentation—the head's turned back. There's no way she could have delivered it like that. I'll try to reposition the dead lamb, and then I'll give her an injection that'll help her to expel it. I'll give her a shot of antibiotics, and that's about all I can do for her." Dan went out to his truck to get the necessary implements.

Dan waited until #169 had successfully birthed the badly bloated stillborn lamb before climbing back into his truck to continue his rounds. Terry buried the lamb, and both of us continued with our chores, feeling grossly inadequate.

We looked in on #169, and she seemed to be feeling somewhat better. Terry and I watched as she ate a few wisps of hay before we left her alone with her surviving lamb.

Two hours later we returned to check again—and found #169 lying dead in the stall. The orphaned lamb lay curled up next to her lifeless body. Both were engulfed in a pool of blood, and we guessed that the mother had suffered a massive, delayed hemorrhage after the stillborn lamb was delivered.

This time we were prepared with bottles, nipples, and milk replacer for the motherless lamb. For the first week or two, we fed her six small bottles of milk replacer daily. As the lamb grew, she needed only three large bottles to get her through the day. She gulped the milk with such zest and enthusiasm that we named her Whiplash, since we feared she would suffer that painful condition from her violent tugs on the nipple.

Over the next few weeks, Tony the alpaca became Whiplash's best friend and dedicated foster parent. Though they seemed an unlikely pair, it was plain to see they were devoted to one another.

Tony

As a child I loved all kinds of animals, and the more un-usual they were, the better I liked them. From toddler-hood, the number-one item on my annual list for Santa Claus was a live monkey. Year after year, I was disappointed when there was no monkey under the tree on Christmas morning. But my dad would take me in his lap and invent a story to ex-plain why, once again, the monkey hadn't materialized.

He didn't say, "You know you can't have a monkey," or "Your mother would never have a monkey in the house," or "Where on earth would we find a monkey?" or anything one might expect a parent to say. Instead he lifted me onto his lap and told a story.

One year he said he could just imagine what must have happened at the North Pole. Santa had indeed received my request for a monkey, and he searched far and wide until he found just the right one. Mrs. Claus got the little monkey dressed in a warm snowsuit, and she set him beside Santa on the seat of the sleigh for the long ride through the night.

"But do you think the monkey would sit still?" Dad asked. "I bet he jumped off the seat, crawled into Santa's bag of toys, and . . ." The tale of the imaginary monkey's antics would go on and on until I was giggling happily and my disappointment was gone.

Even as a young adult, I thought it would be fun to own a monkey. But by the time I had borne three children and survived their preschool years, the idea of a small creature that threw food and swung from chandeliers had begun to lose its appeal for me. I'd been through that already, and I didn't really care to repeat the experience until the grandchildren came along.

I was still fascinated by unusual animals, though, particularly those that could live outside of the house. At the time we bought our first sheep, Terry and I became interested in the alpacas we'd seen at fiber fairs. We were impressed by their gentle natures and their soft, colorful fiber. Natives of South America, alpacas are smaller, less-aggressive cousins of the llama. Alpacas have roamed the foothills of the Andes Mountains for thousands of years. They were domesticated by the Incas, who used their fiber for making clothing and other textiles.

Alpacas communicate with each other and with other species primarily through a form of humming. That hum has a wide variety of tones and expressions, and an alpaca can get its point across in almost any situation. A loud and urgent hum signals danger to other members of the herd, while a quiet, soft hum—almost like a sigh—indicates pleasure or contentment. When an alpaca is curious, its hum sounds like a question: *Hmmmmm?*

We bought two young male alpacas. A high-quality breeding alpaca can cost over ten thousand dollars, so the only affordable option for us was to buy young males that were not destined for breeding. This reduced the price considerably— way down into the two- to three-hundred-dollar range.

We chose a deep auburn-colored alpaca and a black one with a white stripe down his face. Christopher named them Tony and Nigel. Both had some features that were not up to the stringent breed standards—certain particulars of size, markings, or color conformation—and it was stipulated in our sales agreement that they be gelded before they reached breeding age. Still, we felt we made a good deal on some lovely wool producers.

Though they shared a pasture with the sheep, the two alpacas kept entirely to themselves. Alpacas are peaceable animals, and though they tower over the sheep, they will voluntarily step aside as the more tenacious sheep push them out of the way at feeding time.

Tony and Nigel were inseparable. When they lay down to rest, they lay touching, side by side, shaped like two loaves of bread with a long neck and head at either end. This is how alpacas typically rest—in pairs, with a head at each end to watch for danger from all directions. As Tony and Nigel lay side by side they hummed companionably to each other, content in their own little world.

When we had owned them for only a few months, Nigel began exhibiting some strange symptoms. He was growing weaker and he lacked coordination. When the vet came out to see Nigel, he said the condition was caused by a meningeal worm—a parasite that attacks the neurological system. The vet gave him injections to treat the condition, but he said these would do no good if Nigel's case was too far advanced. Though some days Nigel seemed somewhat improved, he steadily declined and soon died.

We weren't sure whether Nigel already had the parasite when we brought him home or whether he picked it up at our farm, but either way it was a bitter disappointment to lose him so soon. Terry, Chris, and I were saddened at Nigel's death, but Tony was devastated. Tony moped around for months, showing no interest in anything. He barely nibbled at his food, eating just enough to sustain his meager existence. Almost a year passed before Tony began to regain some interest in life. Even then, he was never again the completely happy, lighthearted animal he was when Nigel was alive. Tony eventually began to take an interest in the sheep, and though they in no way replaced Nigel in his affections, he learned to tolerate and appreciate their company.

-✳-

About two years after Nigel died, Tony developed a new passion. Lambs. He loved the newborn lambs. Tony's obsession with lambs sometimes clashed with the maternal instincts of the ewes. Tony had a tendency to interfere in the mother-child bonding process when the lambs were newly born. He even learned to recognize the symptoms of a ewe in labor, so he could be close at hand for the birth and be the first to greet the newborn.

The ewes didn't like Tony's interference. When a sheep was in the throes of labor, straining to deliver, the meddlesome Tony could usually be found with his nose only inches from the ewe's raised tail, eagerly awaiting the blessed event.

When the lamb arrived and the ewe was busily working to clean and care for the newborn, Tony's ridiculous fuzzy head was right beside hers, his myopic gaze fixed fondly on the baby.

Alpacas are members of the camelid family, and they do look something like small camels without humps. Within a few years we had more of them, and Tony and his ilk presented an unusual sight in rural Minnesota, where one would more likely expect to see a herd of cows or a flock of sheep. People often stopped their cars to stare at the strange-looking alpacas grazing along the roadside. And the strangest-looking of all the alpacas was Tony.

Tony had a rebellious, wild tuft of reddish brown hair on the top of his head. This tuft was usually adorned with a few wisps of hay or straw, reminiscent of the wooden hairpins of a Japanese geisha. Tony also had a severe case of buck teeth, only in reverse: alpacas have teeth only on their lower jaws, with a hard gum on the top. With the straw-embellished top-knot, luxuriant eyelashes, outlandish underbite, and bulging eyes, Tony was truly a sight to behold.

I don't believe Tony would ever intentionally harm any living thing, but he sometimes couldn't help himself from striking back playfully at the bossy ewes. Occasionally, if he thought no one was watching, Tony set his sights on a distant ewe who was grazing peacefully, minding her own business. With his lurching, clumsy gait, Tony worked himself up to a bouncy gallop, fuzzy head bobbing as he ran. He descended upon the ewe he had selected, reached down, and nipped gently at her well-padded rump. It didn't hurt the ewe, but it did annoy her considerably, which was exactly Tony's goal.

Tony was smart enough to know he would be scolded sternly if he was caught harassing the sheep, so his antics were rarely executed in the presence of humans. But we could usually guess what he had been up to. When he came loping up to the gate to greet us after one of these episodes, the tell-tale signs were there—wisps of wool from his victim's rump were wedged between Tony's hideously protruding teeth.

The orphaned Whiplash was a dream come true for Tony. This was a lamb he could enjoy without suffering the wrath of an overprotective mother. Like Whiplash, Tony grieved the death of a loved one. Tony seemed to understand that Whiplash needed extra care and attention, and throughout the first year of her life he was constantly at her side, watching over her like a buck-toothed guardian angel.

Hunting and gathering

It was the first of April, and Terry began to think about income taxes. One evening, in preparation for his annual capitulation to the demands of the IRS, Terry spent hours closeted with what we loosely termed his "farm accounts." His style of record keeping was not what you'd expect of the professional metrologist. There were no precise columns of figures backed up by relevant documents located in well-organized file folders. That was not how Terry's accounting system operated.

In fact, no attempts were made at record keeping until April fifteenth loomed largely on the horizon. On the first of April Chris and I noticed the onset of the annual phenomenon. On the kitchen table a mountain of loose and random receipts began to accumulate, along with hundreds of crumpled scraps of paper, each bearing some illegible scribble or notation which probably meant something significant at the time it was hastily scrawled.

"Look, Mom. This must be the start of the hunting and

gathering season," said Chris. We watched as Terry searched through a year's worth of old pants and coat pockets. He then braved the clutter on the floor and passenger seat of his pickup truck. Receipts for feed, vet bills, tractor repairs, and auction sale slips were recovered from each of these locations as well as under the refrigerator and in microscopic pieces embedded in the clothes dryer's lint screen.

I normally paid little attention to Terry's annual scramble to organize the financial paperwork for the farming operation. But this was the first time we were going to include the fiber and wool processing as a part of the farm's income, and it dawned on me that Terry's findings might be relevant to my job security as resident shepherdess.

In previous years we considered the exotic animals and wool processing projects hobbies, and we hadn't tracked the related expenses. We knowingly operated at a loss. But if I were to establish a legitimate career as a shepherdess, the financial viability of my activities now mattered.

"I guess I should have been trying harder to earn some money with the animals and the wool," I said to Chris as Terry gathered his piles of receipts and left the room.

Since I'd quit my full-time job, we had sold some lambs, and I'd sold some hand-spun wool and many knitted mittens, but my activities hadn't generated much money. Our primary goal when I quit my job was to free up time for our family to spend together, rather than using all of our daylight hours for work. Terry, Chris, and I all agreed it was great to have me handling the bulk of chores at home, so our evenings were relatively free. I thoroughly enjoyed my months of shepherding and spinning, but I admitted I hadn't given much thought to the financial side of the enterprise.

After hours spent poring over the debits and credits entered on his spreadsheets, Terry emerged from behind the closed door. Armed with a sheaf of papers, he and I sat down at the kitchen table, while Chris played games on the computer nearby.

Terry began his report by saying that not only was our sheep and wool processing venture not very lucrative, it was operating at a serious deficit. "We're going to lose our shirts if we keep on like this," he said.

Chris looked up from his computer game. He wasn't much concerned with financial matters, but this talk about loss of shirts definitely piqued his interest. Even while fully clothed, Terry and I probably registered at the high end of the parent eccentricity scale. Judging from the look on Chris's face, he was wondering how he would explain to his friends the appearance of his mother wandering topless around the sheep yard.

I pulled my attention back to what Terry was saying. It had something to do with dire straits and bottom lines. I was finding it hard to concentrate, and I felt panic rising as I imagined Terry demanding the imminent sale of livestock. What if I had to give up my new career? What if we couldn't afford to keep the animals?

"Not only do the animals not generate much income, they are costing us money. Lots of money," said Terry as he looked up from the columns of figures. "I know you had your heart set on staying home with the animals, but we just can't go on like this."

He leafed through his papers and continued. "If we get rid of the llama and alpaca and cut way back on the sheep and rabbits, we could probably break even with the money we're making now. But there's no way we can afford to keep all of these animals without the income you earned at your old job." Terry concluded his report, and I slumped limply in my chair. It looked like my days as a professional shepherdess were at an end.

Seeing my stunned look, Terry relented slightly. "Let's give it until the end of the year. If you can find a part-time job that'll pay for vet bills and rabbit feed, we'll keep on with this for the rest of the year. If we find we're actually making some money with the wool and the animals, you can quit your job for good. You'll be back to being a full-time shepherdess."

We stayed up late into the night talking. We vowed to start taking the animal and wool enterprise more seriously. We would become professionals, not just hobby farmers. "But if we're going to keep going, we need to do it in a more business-like way," Terry said. "We can't go on operating at a loss."

As we talked our plans became more and more grand. We would take our breeding lambs to shows where they would win prizes and bring top dollar at the sales. We would advertise both the breeding stock and the hand-spun and hand-knit woolen products in trade publications and on the Internet. I would work more craft fairs, where I would sell huge quantities of spun yarn and hand-knit mittens at exorbitant prices.

Months earlier, our son Jon had offered to help us design a website to promote the animals and wool products. We would take him up on his offer and start some serious marketing.

Terry and I made an agreement. If, at the end of the year, the farm was still operating at a loss, we would sell most of the livestock and discontinue the wool processing venture and I'd go back to full-time work off the farm. But for the time being, I would find a part-time job to earn enough to keep the enterprise afloat while continuing to act as head shepherdess.

I agreed to the ultimatum, but deep inside I knew no matter what the numbers said I couldn't bear to let go. It was too late. I had fallen deeply and irreversibly in love with the farm and the animals—the whole lifestyle. There was no turning back. Somehow we'd have to make the shepherding business profitable.

The office

Over the next few days I scanned the want ads in the local newspaper, looking for a fairly lucrative part-time job that would allow me the time and flexibility to oversee the flock. It didn't take me long to realize those jobs were few and far between.

One day when I was feeling particularly discouraged, I got a phone call from Pat, a man with whom I had worked on several projects at my last full-time job. Pat was a self-employed grants management consultant, and he suggested I might be able to find similar work. After quitting my job, I had done some occasional grant writing on a contract basis to help ease the financial transition from full-time employment to full-time shepherdess. But I hadn't seriously considered doing this work long term.

"You've been writing grant applications for years, and I know you've developed some great relationships in the public sector," Pat said. "Here's your chance to make use of those connections. Besides, you'll be offering a service that's really needed in rural areas."

After giving the idea some consideration, I decided to try it. It was a big step for me, when after fifteen years of working for agencies in the nonprofit sector, I ventured out on my own as a self-employed grant writer and grants management consultant. My first job was working with Pat on a municipal water tower and housing rehabilitation project. I wrote the portion of the grant application dealing with home repairs for low-income residents of a nearby town, while Pat addressed the city's need for a new water tower and sewer system.

This arrangement made sense for me. I could work on my home computer most of the time, since most of my projects involved writing and Internet-based research. It was interesting to collaborate with small towns on developing solutions to their problems and helping them access state and federal grant money to build and repair homes, roads, and water towers.

I was disappointed that I couldn't devote myself totally to the sheep and the farm, but the prospect of working at home, surrounded by family and animals, definitely beat that of the daily grind at an office. And besides, it was only temporary. I vowed to be back to full-time shepherding by the end of the year.

In the first few months of self-employment, my main concern was generating enough grant writing business to replace some of the income I'd earned at my previous job. I didn't want to invest money in office furniture and equipment that would be abandoned when I returned to full-time shepherding.

In the bay window of our living room, I improvised an office. I set up a flimsy card table for my files and research manuals. A tiny, cluttered desk held our outdated family computer, which served as my writing and Internet research center. The same computer still served as Chris's video game station, so during my work hours I angled the monitor away from his various car-racing accessories: the joystick, the big black steering wheel, the accelerator pedal.

Despite the outlandish setup, working at home had some distinct advantages. At my previous job I was expected to dress and behave somewhat appropriately, while at home the minimum standards were far less exacting. On most days I dressed in an old T-shirt and sweatpants, eating Triscuits out of the box as I worked at the computer.

Though it wasn't the same as being a full-time shepherd-ess and wool spinner, I loved the freedom to walk out to visit the sheep at any time of the day. I could make hourly trips to the sheep shed to check for newborns during spring lambing. Compared to the years when both Terry and I left for work early in the morning, this was a real improvement.

I was never lonely working at home: three house cats were there to keep me company. They were invaluable as paper-weights to hold down the reams of documents piled on my makeshift card table desk. I did my best to maintain a lively discussion with the cats as they lay sleeping on the card table or on the floor nearby.

"How's your day going, Luigi?" I asked the youngest. "Do you have anything important on your calendar today?"

Luigi rolled over onto his back with all four feet pointed skyward, his paws dangling loosely, and replied with a drawn-out *"mrrrrrooooow."*

One day, I'd been directing endless comments, observa-tions, and unanswered questions to what I assumed to be Mrs. Tinkles, lying curled up in a corner of the living room. When she hadn't moved by late afternoon, I went to check for signs of life. I had mistaken an old black sweatshirt for her obese, slatternly form.

I found both positive and negative aspects to having cats

as one's only business associates. Opinions may be expressed freely, without fear of offending anyone or appearing politically incorrect. The cats either ignored or slept through even the worst of insults, and they tolerated bad jokes and petty criticisms well. Gone was the danger of offending thin-skinned co-workers with thoughtless comments. The downside was the cats made absolutely no effort to share the workload.

Moreover, they monopolized my card table desk. At any given time, two cats were stationed on top of the table, and the third cat was never far away. The card table was an ideal perch from which to gaze out the window at passing birds or to look scornfully down at the cat lying on the floor below. But there were a few problems with this arrangement. When a bird was spotted through the window or the corpulent form of Mrs. Tinkles passed by below, the two cats on the table were likely to launch themselves abruptly off the cluttered surface, scattering papers, pens, and files. I can't count the times I had to explain the presence of claw holes in legal affidavits, property deeds, and city council resolutions.

My work load increased, and the card table took on a slightly swaybacked appearance as it bent under the weight of thick files and heavy research manuals, not to mention the overweight cats. On the floor surrounding the card table were cardboard boxes overflowing with file folders and paperwork. Soon the whole living room floor was littered with work-related papers, binders, and books.

When we were expecting company, I went into a cleaning frenzy. I dragged the cardboard boxes away and folded up the card table. It was a major undertaking to dismantle and reassemble what we began to refer to as *the office* on these occasions. The Thanksgiving and Christmas holidays caused the greatest disruption. We set up our Christmas tree in the bay window, so when the holidays rolled around, I had to close the office for a month.

Everyone in the family had to make some major adjustments when I began working at home. My presence in the living room sometimes caused a conflict with those who wanted to watch television there. It was not much of a problem during the week, when I had the house to myself most of the time. But during school vacations, I struggled to maintain any semblance of order at the office.

It was partly an image problem. All too often I'd be on an important phone call to a client or a state agency when Chris yelled, "That's too much, Bob!" in response to a contestant's bid on *The Price Is Right*. It was also hard to maintain the illusion of professionalism during a client phone call when a ferocious cat fight erupted on my card table or a lamb— warming itself in a cardboard box by the oven door—bleated loudly.

Chris became an unpaid and unwilling receptionist, file clerk, and general domestic servant. Early on it became apparent that he was not cut out for office work, but no one else was available for the position. I encouraged him to let my work-related phone calls go to the answering machine when I was outside tending the sheep. Then I could be reasonably certain that a somewhat decipherable message would be waiting for me when I returned to the house. But Chris rarely missed an opportunity to answer the phone. After all, it might be one of his friends calling.

One afternoon I came inside after feeding the livestock. Chris was engrossed in a car racing game on the Xbox. Without taking his eyes off the screen he said, "Some lady called for you while you were outside."

"Did you take a message?"

"No. I . . . well . . . actually, I guess I hung up on her."

In response to my stern look, he squirmed uncomfortably, "I was in the middle of a race! I would have lost it if I'd put down the controller to take a message."

This kind of thing was not good for public relations. The problem could have been solved by installing a separate phone line for the consulting business, but I was in no hurry to do anything so permanent. Like the office, the business itself was of a transient nature.

I contracted for work on a project-by-project basis, and when one job ended, another one might or might not be waiting. Sometimes I was flooded with more consulting work than I could handle, but just as often there were lean times when I was between jobs.

Just as Chris became the office's reluctant aide-de-camp, I assumed the dual roles of shepherdess-CEO, trying to function simultaneously in two totally different universes. The fast-paced business world often collided with the pastoral realm, and we all felt the impact.

❋

One cold and stormy April morning, shortly after initiating the joint ventures of self-employed consultant and shepherdess, I was expecting an important phone call from the HUD office in Washington about a pending grant application. A few last ewes were about to lamb, and I carried my cell phone with me on my frequent trips to the shed to check on them.

Upon counting heads in the sheep shed, I discovered one very pregnant ewe was missing from the flock. Hmm, I thought. She must have slipped outside. The shed door was kept open slightly to provide a measure of ventilation and light, and the sheep—if they were determined or foolish enough—could squeeze through. Though they rarely venture outside in freezing or stormy weather, a ewe will sometimes leave the flock and the shed, seeking privacy during her labor and delivery.

I bundled up warmly and trudged out to the snowy pasture to look for the missing ewe. After nearly an hour of trekking across the bitterly cold landscape through knee-deep snow drifts, I spotted the mother-to-be. The ewe had chosen to give birth on a windswept hillside almost half a mile from the warm, dry sheep shed.

By the time I reached the ewe, I could see the birth was imminent. Dropping to my knees beside her, I was just in time to catch the wet and steaming lamb before it landed on the frozen, snow-covered ground.

Instinctively, I felt compelled to gather the newborn into my arms and rush it back to the warmth and safety of the sheep shed. But when a lamb is taken from its mother right after its birth, the mother will sometimes refuse to claim and care for the baby when it is reintroduced to her later—as was the case with Lamb Chop. I wanted to give the ewe enough time with her new baby that she'd remember the lamb after I concealed it inside my warm coat and carried it back to the shed.

Working quickly to clear the amniotic sac away from the lamb's nose and mouth, I positioned the baby on my lap within reach of its mother so she could begin bonding with it immediately. The ewe sniffed and licked the small face before emitting that familiar chuckling sound all shepherds love to hear—that odd rumbling communication from ewe to newborn lamb denoting the mother's recognition and acceptance of her baby.

At that instant my cell phone erupted loudly in its cheerful melody, signaling the phone call from HUD—another moment of critical importance. Frantically searching through numerous coat pockets with my free hand, I located the phone and answered it. On the blustery hillside I crouched beside the ewe, the icy wind whipping around us. With the cell phone clutched in one stiff hand, I negotiated the terms of a contract with a disembodied voice in far-off Washington, while cradling a wet and shivering newborn lamb in the other arm. The ewe, her breath escaping in steamy wisps into the frigid air, was oblivious to my conversation as she nuzzled and licked the lamb. She was busy immersing herself in the unique scent and taste and texture of her baby.

After concluding the contract negotiations, I struggled with numb fingers to return the cell phone to my pocket. That feat accomplished, I shoved my hands into my wool-lined leather mittens and began the long walk back to the sheep shed.

Ted, Mr. Johnson, and the flood

Farming and shepherding tasks are dictated by the rhythm of the seasons and the vagaries of nature. The planting and harvesting of crops; the breeding, lambing, and shearing of sheep—all of these are part of the organic flow of activities that naturally blend into the seasons' progression. Birth, growth, and reproduction; life and death—all happen in their own time and season.

The day-to-day life of the shepherd with a small flock hasn't changed significantly over the past two thousand years. I spent a large part of my days walking over the hills and through the woods, checking on the health and welfare of the flock and tending to its needs. Following the age-old shepherd's routine was like tapping into the very essence of life. All the unnecessary waste and hurry and turmoil of modern existence were pared away, leaving a soothing balm of fundamental well-being.

This harmonious state contrasted sharply with the fast-paced, high-tech world of government grants management into which I'd been catapulted. My consulting work was usually challenging, sometimes exhilarating, and often stressful. I was driven by relentless bureaucratic and seemingly arbitrary deadlines. When not up against a specific deadline, I sometimes spent entire days filling out endless copies of government forms to be submitted quarterly, in triplicate. The never-ending paperwork was a real pain, and it seemed that every page of each report required excruciating detail. Nearly every week there were new procedures, new forms, new regulations with which to comply, and these changes required frequent upgrades in technology.

We reluctantly decided to upgrade from our old dial-up Internet service to a wireless provider. But the wireless companies in our area couldn't provide service because of our remote location. Our only option was to install a huge, ugly antenna on our roof to receive a signal from a transmitter tower on a hilltop miles away.

Two technicians spent an entire afternoon mounting and adjusting the wiry behemoth on the roof. The sheep were wary of this new development. Rosie, Ada, and the others watched as the skeletal object began to take shape. One by one, the sheep stopped grazing. They gathered curiously along the fenceline to watch the proceedings. Unblinking, thirty sets of eyes followed the men as they walked back and forth from van to house and up and down the ladder.

When the job was done, the men loaded their equipment into the van and drove away. The sheep continued to stare at the house for a long while. For the next few days the entire flock seemed to be watching and waiting for additional alien life-forms to alight on the roof in response to whatever invisible signal was being transmitted.

By the end of April, the pace of my consulting work had picked up considerably. There were no more lazy days of sitting at home with the cats, spinning wool, or doing routine paperwork at my card table.

One might assume that the working hours of a grant writer/grants management consultant are spent sitting safely in a climate-controlled office, far from the scene of any action. That was not the case for my fledgling enterprise. My workdays were sometimes fraught with danger, intrigue, and suspense. Two of the most extreme hazards proved to be disgruntled clients and natural disasters. I had the misfortune to encounter both in the course of one long day that April.

❋

The day was darkly overcast with occasional gusty winds. Over four inches of rain had fallen overnight, contributing to a rapid snowmelt, and towns to the west of our farm were flooding. Western Minnesota is prairie country, with small towns scattered across a mostly flat landscape. I listened closely to the news and weather reports before going outside to do my morning sheep chores. Two of the western Minnesota communities threatened by flooding were my clients.

Lately, my consulting work had evolved: in addition to grant writing, I was now administering a grant-funded housing rehabilitation program that helped residents of a poor, rural county make repairs to their homes, and I had appointments that morning with three homeowners on the western edge of the state.

One, a typical participant, was an elderly widow, living alone. Her only income came from Social Security, and it was less than $6,000 a year. She could barely afford to live on that income, let alone update her old electrical system or reshingle her roof. The roof had been leaking for years, and finally the ceilings were starting to collapse. Deteriorating rapidly, the home had become a health and safety hazard. The county public health department asked for help from our program.

It was a good match: the program's purpose was to reha-
bilitate homes such as these. The elderly widow's roof would
be shingled, the ceilings repaired, the electrical system up-
graded, and other updates made to the plumbing and heating
systems. When the work was finished, the home would provide a safe and secure dwelling for the woman as long as she
lived there, and after that, it would be a good solid home for
another family. A lien was recorded against the property so
that when the home was eventually sold the grant program
would be repaid. The repayment would then be used to repair
another home.

Without programs such as these, many homes in rural
communities fall into disrepair because the owners can't afford to maintain them. After a decade or two of neglect, most
houses deteriorate beyond repair. And once those existing
homes are gone, the cost to replace them with new construction is prohibitive for local residents. Eventually, a housing
shortage develops, and without adequate housing, new families are not attracted to the area, population declines, and rural communities dwindle and die.

Many of the old houses in western Minnesota still have
their original wiring from the 1930s and '40s, when the only
demands on the electrical system were a few lights and a ra-
dio. In winter, it's still common to find low-income people using old, unsafe electrical and propane space heaters scattered
throughout their homes. It's a disaster waiting to happen, and
it seems every winter at least one fatal house fire in our area
is caused by improper use of space heaters combined with an
overloaded electrical system.

These programs leverage tax dollars in ways that pay back.
They help elderly and disadvantaged people to stay in their
homes, which is far more cost-effective than moving them
into nursing homes or building more subsidized rental units.
The programs address whatever is a problem: they remove

lead paint hazards from the homes of young children, improve accessibility in the homes of elderly and handicapped people, and preserve affordable housing. They enhance the local tax base, and ultimately, they save rural communities. These housing rehabilitation programs were some of my favorite consulting projects because they simply made sense. I almost didn't mind the huge volume of paperwork they required.

-*-

Though my grant writing activities were usually hazard-free, grants administration could get hairy. Most of the homeowners—like the elderly widow—were cooperative, pleasant, and very grateful for the program's assistance. It was difficult to come away from a home visit without a plate of freshly baked cookies or some other homemade gift forced into one's hands. But sometimes disputes arose between construction crews, dissatisfied property owners, and project management. When tempers escalated, situations could turn nasty. Such was the case with the other two appointments I had that morning.

Arriving at the home of a low-income couple who needed help in working through a misunderstanding with a construction company, I saw the contractor's truck already parked beside the house. I rummaged through my mobile filing cabinet—i.e., plastic milk crate—and located the file for the Arnegaard home repair project.

The thick stack of incident reports already in the file outlined the Arnegaards' history of disagreements with the contractor who had been hired to repair their home. As I stepped out of my car, I heard slamming doors and loud, angry voices. Things were not going to go well.

I climbed the three steps leading to the front entrance and raised my fist to knock on the outer door. The screen door flew open, missing my nose by mere inches. In the doorway stood the man of the house, wearing a crazed look in his eye and little else. The small, wiry man was shirtless, and he wore a tattered kilt-like undergarment. I didn't get a good look at the unique outfit because he was leaping and twirling madly about the room. Judging from what I could see of the face beneath his bushy, foot-long beard, he was about sixty years old.

The Charles Manson lookalike held a steak knife in his unsteady hand. He paused in his swirling, leaping dance long enough to grasp my right arm, yanking me roughly into the house. Once inside, he maintained his viselike grip on my wrist. All of the window blinds were closed, and though it was midmorning, the room was almost totally dark.

"Let her go, Ted!" a woman's voice yelled from somewhere inside the dark house.

But Ted wasn't ready to let go. Ted was stronger than he looked, and in one quick, fluid move, he pinned my arm behind my back, bent me over his kilted knee, and fixed the serrated edge of his knife against my throat. Ted thrust his grizzled face to within inches of mine and spat, "Gotcha, you damn socialist!" He pressed the blade hard against my jugular. The blunt edge pushed deeply into my flesh. The pressure alone didn't break the skin, but now Ted raised his elbow as if to draw the knife across my throat.

Then he was gone. After what felt like an eternity bent backward over his bony knee, I was able to breathe, and I struggled to my feet.

Mrs. Arnegaard had seized Ted from behind, and she effortlessly lifted his rancid, near-naked weight off me. Ted's better half was a far more substantial individual than her husband, and she disarmed him easily.

Acting as though nothing unusual had happened, Mrs. Arnegaard hauled Ted along as she graciously showed me into her kitchen, where she, the contractor, and I were able to resolve the construction-related dispute. Throughout our discussion, as we sat decorously around the kitchen table, Mrs. Arnegaard held her thrashing, cursing, purple-faced husband in a firm headlock.

"How about a cup of coffee?" Mrs. Arnegaard suggested to the contractor and me when our business was finished.

"Oh! Look at the time! Sorry—I'd love to stay, but I really need to get to my next appointment." Both the contractor and I stammered out excuses as we backed our way to the door. Neither of us dared turn our back on the barbarous gaze of Ted, whose head was still tightly wedged between the doughy arm and ample bosom of his wife.

Leaving the Arnegaards' house, I collapsed in my car, weak-kneed and still shaking after the close call with Ted and his steak knife. I jotted a note to myself to draft yet another incident report for the Arnegaard file.

I needed to make a phone call before my next appointment, but I didn't want to stay parked outside the Arnegaard home any longer than necessary. A few miles down the gravel road, I pulled over and glanced into the rearview mirror, half expecting the tartan-clan avenger to appear over the top of the hill, swinging a machete.

Paging through my notes, I searched for the phone number of a heating contractor who had installed a furnace for another homeowner. I was hoping to meet with the contractor and homeowner to mediate a long-standing dispute.

Roy Johnson—an elderly, handicapped man—had called me several times in the past weeks to complain about the furnace that had been installed through our program. He said after the new furnace had been put in, his home often dipped below freezing temperatures at night, even with the thermostat cranked up to 85 degrees. Certainly, he said, something must be wrong with the furnace.

I had never met Mr. Johnson in person, but judging from our many phone conversations, I pictured him as a sweet, defenseless old man. I hated to imagine him sitting in a cold house because of the contractor's refusal to repair or replace the furnace.

But when I called the contractor to get his side of the story, he swore the furnace was operating perfectly. He said that he and his employees had met with the homeowner and checked the furnace many times, yet they were not able to satisfy the man. Each time, the contractor claimed, it appeared that Roy had been fiddling with the thermostat or adjusting some dial or other, causing the furnace to malfunction. When the repairmen reset the controls, the furnace would kick in and work fine. But still Roy complained. He claimed the furnace was a worthless piece of junk, and it didn't provide enough warmth to heat a henhouse.

The contractor told me, "There's nothing wrong with the furnace, but there sure as hell is something wrong with that old man. The guy is crazy. My installers are afraid to go out there again."

How could that be? I immediately slipped into my advocate mode and rushed to the homeowner's defense. "Certainly he can't be that bad! He's nearly ninety years old and uses a walker. What can your crew be afraid of?"

I'd left quite a few phone messages for the contractor, asking him to try once more to make things right for Mr. Johnson. I told him what time I'd arrive at Roy's place, and asked him to meet me there, too. Surely we could resolve the problem through a face-to-face meeting.

But for some reason the contractor wasn't returning my calls. After leaving the Arnegaards' I tried calling him one more time. Finally, he answered.

"Can you meet me at Roy Johnson's place in half an hour?" I asked.

"Forget it!" He said. "I'm not setting foot over there again, and if you have any sense, you won't go either."

"But I've already set up the appointment! He's expecting us both to show up."

"Well, you're on your own. If you're still determined to go over there, take my advice. Sneak around to the back door. Don't walk right up the sidewalk to the front door, because he'll see you coming."

"Oh, come on now! He's an old man. You've got to be kidding!"

"Just take my advice. Don't let him get a clear shot at you."

I continued on my way, sincerely hoping the contractor's comment was just a bad joke.

Mr. Johnson lived in the wilds of western Minnesota. It took me half an hour to get there from the Arnegaard place, and the directions Roy had given me were pretty sketchy. I drove up and down winding gravel roads, looking for some sign or landmark to indicate I was nearing the Johnson place. He had said his home was on a hilltop, at the end of a mile-long driveway. I slowed the car to a crawl in the area where I expected to find the turnoff, wondering if I had made a wrong turn somewhere. Then I rounded a sharp curve and saw a long dirt track snaking up a steep hill.

I knew without a doubt I had found the right place when I spotted something lying at the base of the hill, blocking the driveway. It was a twisted, smoldering heap of sheet metal riddled with bullet holes. Roy's new furnace, exactly as he had described it. A worthless piece of junk.

Just then my cell phone rang. It was Doris, the city clerk of Mansfield. "Did you hear about the flooding?" she asked. "How soon can you get over here?"

My heart sank at the prospect of yet another stressful adventure, but at the same time I was relieved to have an excuse to postpone my visit with dear old Mr. Johnson.

❖

Just after I started my consulting business, I landed a job writing grants for Mansfield, a small Minnesota village that had no formal office facilities. The only city-owned building in town was the municipal liquor store, and I kept the grant project's administrative records in a filing cabinet in the back room behind the bar. There, in a clearing amidst cases of whiskey, vodka, and wine coolers, I sat at a desk consisting of a wooden plank on top of an empty beer keg.

When Terry's friends asked him how my consulting business was going, he entertained them with tales of his wife sitting at a municipal liquor store two days a week. He didn't bother to explain that I was working on my grant files in the back room.

Mansfield sometimes flooded when there were heavy rains and a rapid snow melt. The streams and rivers along Minnesota's western border flood frequently in the spring, leaving homes damaged or destroyed, roads washed out, and towns stranded for days at a time. The citizens of Mansfield were used to coping with the inconvenience of temporary road closures and wet basements, but this year there were dire predictions that the flooding was going to be worse than usual.

That's what Doris, the city clerk, told me when she called that morning. "Can you get over here right away?" she asked. "The water's rising fast, and it looks like the whole south end of town is going under. If you could pick up your grant files, you can work from home until the water goes down."

Normally, Mansfield is just over a half-hour's drive west from Roy Johnson's place. But that day, it took me nearly two hours to get there. As I neared the state's western border, I was forced to zigzag across the countryside, hitting dead ends where the roads disappeared into swirling floodwaters. Each time that happened, I had to backtrack and try another route.

The water was rising so quickly that the county highway crews couldn't keep up. They weren't able to mark or blockade all the flooded roads, so drivers traveled at their own risk. The farther west I drove, the less traffic I met. Eventually, the sparse traffic dwindled away completely. I had met no other cars on the road for more than ten miles.

Speeding down the abandoned highway, I finally reached a point where it seemed all of the main roads heading west were impassable. Taking a chance, I headed south on a narrow gravel track, hoping to find a minor road that might still be open to the west.

At first, my race with the rising floodwaters was exhilarating, and the adrenaline rush kept my spirits up. But about two miles down the gravel track, I came to a stop, overcome by a sick feeling of apprehension.

As far as the eye could see, there was water. Looking into my rearview mirror, I saw that the water that had been lapping at the grass verge a moment ago now completely covered the road. The road in front of me was covered by a rippling current. Its depth was difficult to gauge, since the entire surrounding landscape was submerged. It could be six inches of water, or six feet. There were no telephone poles, no road ditches, nor any road signs visible. It was virtually impossible to judge the depth of the ever-expanding lake.

All around me, in every direction, were dark expanses of angry, churning water. Then—to top it all off—the gray and sullen clouds overhead split open. Fat raindrops plopped onto my windshield and obscured the surroundings, which actually didn't matter, since nothing but water was visible in any direction.

Driving in western Minnesota, one can go for miles without seeing any signs of civilization. My cell phone was useless; it had no service west of Hoffman. I was stranded between two submerged stretches of gravel road with the water still rising. My chances of being rescued were slim, since no one knew exactly where I was, and I feared I would be stranded for days. Or worse—drowned.

After sitting in the car for a few minutes, thinking over the situation, I realized there were no good alternatives. I made a decision.

I shifted into drive, and the car crawled forward. Gusts of wind rocked the vehicle and sent whitecaps racing across the watery surface of the landscape. Wave after wave washed over the hood and up onto the windshield, but the car kept moving slowly forward. Miraculously, the engine didn't stall, and the car stayed on the invisible roadway.

I inched along for about a quarter of a mile this way. Midway through that nerve-racking voyage, I thought I could see solid ground ahead. Like a mirage appearing between passes of the windshield wipers, the shape of a gravel path emerged from the wall of water ahead. I nearly wept when a dry stretch of road rose up to meet the car's tires.

Huge waves of relief washed over me as the car climbed onto solid ground. I had happened upon a segment of the road that was not yet submerged, and from there I could reach Mansfield.

The town's main street was covered by axle-deep water, but it was still passable. I parked the car and waded across the street to the municipal liquor store. Inside I gathered up the files I would need to manage the grant program from home. As I was piling the last folders into a box, water rippled over the threshold of the building and fanned out across the floor.

I met Doris on the main street as I was carrying my final load to the car. "Did you get all the grant files?" she asked.

I nodded. The rain pelted down hard on us, and the wind nearly took my breath away.

"Great. Good job," said Doris. "Now get out of here."

"I can't just leave you here to deal with all of this." I

gestured toward the mountain of water-soaked boxes and piles of city records still sitting on the curb.

"You'll do us a lot more good if you get those grant files to a safe place and keep the program up and running." She sent me on my way with a firm admonishment: "I mean it. Get out of here while you can."

As always, the citizens of Mansfield bore the flooding stoically. Though it was rarely a life-threatening situation, the near-annual flooding caused a huge mess and massive property damage.

A deputy sheriff's car cruised slowly down the water-logged main street. I waved him down and asked, "Are there any roads open going east?"

"Yeah. If you leave right now, you should be able to get out on twenty-seven."

"Thanks!" I yelled. I sincerely wished I'd known that earlier.

I waded back to the car and drove slowly out of the ever-expanding lake that was downtown Mansfield, heading east toward home.

Rosie's twins

It was the last day of April, and everyone had lambed except for Rosie. When I went out to check the sheep that morning, she stood alone in the shed, looking mournfully up at me.

The other sheep were outside in the bright sunlight, grazing on the new spears of green grass that were poking through the old brown stubble. The lambs were frolicking about the pasture, running in circles and leaping high over imaginary obstacles. Only Rosie, her body swollen and graceless, was left inside.

I finished my morning chores and was about to leave the shed when Rosie let out a dramatic sigh. I knelt down beside her to take a closer look. Her eyes glazed over, and she pawed the ground restlessly. She had the sway-backed, hollow-sided appearance of a ewe whose lamb has dropped in preparation for birth.

"Rosie, it looks like today might be the day," I said as I guided her into a lambing pen. I filled a bucket with water for her and spread fresh straw in the pen. Her labor was not too far advanced, and I was sure I had time to walk out to get the mail at the end of the driveway before Rosie would be ready to deliver.

By the time I returned to the sheep shed, Rosie had already given birth to twins, a moorit ram lamb and a strawberry ewe lamb. Shetland sheep occasionally produce one of these pinkish lambs. They turn completely white within a month, but they provide an interesting variation in the parade of black, white, and brown babies that arrive routinely during lambing season.

I shooed the ever-present Tony away and bent to examine the new lambs. Both were already on their feet, taking their first awkward steps. The male was bright and alert, but Rosie's little strawberry just didn't seem quite normal. She appeared healthy enough, and her condition was good. Something was not quite right, but I couldn't put my finger on it.

Mulling over the mystery of Rosie's ewe lamb, I went back to the house for lunch. After taking off my coat and boots, I walked through the kitchen and living room on my way to the bathroom to wash up. Just in time, I remembered to stop and look for Luigi on top of the seven-foot-tall antique dresser that stood in the living room. There he was, lurking again. I could barely see the tips of his black ears over the scrollwork. Far too many times I'd forgotten to check to see if he was there, and he scared the daylights out of me when he dropped onto my back or shoulders as I passed by. Luigi meant no harm—it was a favorite game—but his unexpected ambushes have probably taken years off my life.

"Luigi!" I scolded. "Come down from there right now."

The black ear tips remained motionless above the edge of the dresser.

"Luigi, come down!"

When he could stand the suspense no longer, Luigi's small

black and white face rose above the dresser's edge just high enough to expose his luminous green eyes.

"I see you, so you might as well come down," I said. "You're going to have to find someone else to ambush. It's not going to be me this time."

Luigi rose from his crouched position and effortlessly sprang from his towering perch to the floor. He followed me into the bathroom, where he batted a paw at the stream of water flowing from the faucet as I washed my hands.

Luigi trailed along behind me when I went back to the kitchen. I don't spend much time there: cooking and housework are not my strong suits. I would rather trim the toenails of an angry llama on a hot day than stay inside in the air conditioning to cook a meal or dust the furniture. As a result, the house is often a mess and the menu selections are limited.

I set two slices of bread and a can of tuna on the kitchen counter and reached for the can opener. From my vantage point near the sink, I could see Mr. and Mrs. Tinkles sprawled across the living room floor like throw rugs. They looked dead to the world, and I thought I might possibly be able to eat my lunch in peace.

But the sound of the electric can opener served as an alarm clock. Both sleeping cats woke instantly, and they rushed to join Luigi at my feet. All three wound themselves around my ankles, making it hard for me to move without stepping on their feet or tails. They knew food was involved, so they were on their best behavior—purring, rubbing against my legs, looking up expectantly.

Mr. Tinkles especially enjoyed my kitchen-table lunches. In fact, an elaborate game had evolved for the occasion. One day as I sat down to eat my lunch, Mr. Tinkles jumped up and lay down beside my bowl of soup. I nudged him to the floor, saying, "No, kitty." This was no deterrent, and he was immediately back in position on the table, sniffing delicately at the steaming bowl. After a few failed attempts to keep the cat's face out of my lunch, I spotted Chris's toy Nerf gun lying on the counter. The plastic gun could shoot soft foam balls in rapid succession, like a machine gun. I grabbed the weapon and leveled it at Mr. Tinkles. He sensed no danger and continued to hover over the bowl, his tongue fully extended, ready to begin lapping up the savory broth. His eyes were half closed in anticipation.

One green foam ball hit him squarely on the shoulder, and he jumped in surprise. The ball didn't hurt him, but it got his attention. Tinkles's ears lay flat against his head and his tail lashed the air as he crouched over the soup bowl. Three more shots sent him diving off the table and galloping from the room.

It became our daily lunchtime routine. I sat at the table with the Nerf gun at my right hand. Tinkles sprang to the table and edged toward my plate, and I aimed the weapon at him in warning. He gave me a look that clearly said, "Bring it on!" as he continued to advance on my food. I then commenced to empty the gun with a barrage of foam balls raining over the cat as he scampered from the room. Moments later, he returned and we repeated the whole exercise again. Mr. Tinkles grew to anticipate our violent game even more than he lusted after my chicken noodle soup. If I didn't start shooting at him as soon as I sat down at the table, he reached up and nudged the gun with his paw, urging me to take action.

But that day my thoughts were on Rosie and her new lambs as I made my tuna sandwich. Just as I sat down at the kitchen table, the phone rang. I set the sandwich down and picked up the phone.

"You won't believe what that damn dog has done now!" shouted the unidentified caller.

"Luan?" I asked.

"Who else do you know who's got an old black dog that's ruining her life?"

"What has he done this time?" I couldn't imagine what Tux could possibly have added to his long list of misdeeds. He had already eaten the upholstery off Luan's furniture, vomited on her new carpet, and nearly murdered Stella the rabbit more times than I could count.

Meanwhile, Mr. Tinkles had returned to the kitchen and was growing impatient. He eyed my sandwich, then batted at the Nerf gun, trying to get my attention. I lifted the weapon and fired a few rounds at him. He ran into the living room, looking over his shoulder, clearly hoping I would follow with the gun.

"He bit me!" exclaimed Luan.

"What! Tux bit you? I can't believe it!" I was astounded. Tux was crazy and unpredictable, but he was utterly devoted to Luan.

"Well, you know how cold it's been at night lately," Luan began. "I've been using my electric blanket, since the furnace is on the fritz. And Tux figured out long ago that the warmest place in the house is in my bed. So guess where he sleeps?" Luan did not pause for an answer. "That's right. You guessed it. Right in the middle of my bed. He hogs the entire mattress, and he barely leaves me any room at the very edge. I've fallen onto the floor more than once."

Meanwhile, Mr. Tinkles was stoked and eager for battle. He stood broadside at the kitchen door, cracking his long tail like a whip, intentionally making himself an easy target. I reloaded and fired another volley.

"There! Gotcha!" My shout of triumph was matched by the rapid-fire mechanism of the gun.

"What *are* you doing?" demanded Luan.

"I just shot the cat."

"Good. You had too many of them anyway." Without missing a beat, she continued, "Not only that, Tux twitches and snores all night. My back is *positively raw* from the scratching."

Tux's toenails were brutal. I'd seen them. Luan was too soft-hearted to make Tux sleep on the floor, and his nocturnal thrashing had left her with more than a few bruises.

"Well, now he's figured out how warm it is under the electric blanket. He knows I turn it on just before I brush my teeth at night. So when he sees me go into the bathroom at bedtime, he burrows down under the covers and lies perfectly still. He thinks I don't see him. Last night when I came out of the bathroom and got into bed, the damn thing bit me!"

"So what did you do?" I asked.

"I slept on the couch, of course," she answered as if it were completely natural to let a small, elderly dog attack you and commandeer your bed. I winced as Luan slammed down the receiver. Our phone conversations were all like this. They rarely began or ended in a conventional manner.

Tinkles appeared again in the doorway, his back arched and tail boldly waving, daring me to make his day.

❋

When Terry got home from work that afternoon, I brought him out to the shed to see Rosie's lambs. He agreed: something was peculiar about the strawberry ewe lamb, even though her little tummy was taut and full of milk, and she seemed to have the normal instincts of a healthy newborn.

As the days went by, more specific manifestations of the lamb's oddness cropped up. Most newborns are content to stay under the heat lamp in their lambing pen, and they have no desire to venture far from their mothers. But Rosie's ewe lamb was not satisfied to stay in the pen with her mother and twin brother. Again and again, she squeezed herself through a gap in the lower boards of the pen and wandered away. Sometimes she left the sheep shed altogether and wandered far out into the farmyard. Restless and wandering newborns are usually not getting enough milk, especially those belonging to sets of twins or triplets. But Rosie's twins always had full bellies, and we knew they were well fed.

During the next few days Terry, Chris, and I rescued the lamb repeatedly from various locations around the yard. In honor of her wandering nature, Terry christened her Rambling Rose.

At first, we weren't too worried about her behavioral quirks. But within a week we noticed that Rambling Rose was lagging far behind her brother developmentally. Her movements were odd and uncoordinated. We suspected that she might have been injured during one of her early rambling sessions, or she may have been deprived of oxygen during her birth.

Then, at the one-week mark, Rambling Rose's most serious problem came to light. Terry had put out the evening's ration of hay for the sheep. We finished our chores and were leaning against the upper planks of the nearest lambing pen, watching the ewes lined up around the hay feeders, munching away.

As we looked on, Rambling Rose once again made her escape through the bottom boards of the lambing pen. She blundered aimlessly around the shed, narrowly missing sheep legs and feeders. Then she ran head-on into a wall.

"Did you see that?"

"It looks almost as if she's blind," Terry said.

Terry walked to where Rose stood, shaking her head in confusion after her abrupt encounter with the shed wall, and he lifted the lamb into his arms. As he held her, I moved my hands in front of her face, looking for a reaction. Rose was completely oblivious, but at the same time she seemed to be intently listening to the sounds around her.

"Set her down again," I suggested, "and let's see what happens."

Terry set the strawberry lamb on her feet in the middle of the shed. Frightened by all the unexpected attention, Rose took off at full speed, bouncing off a wall and a hay feeder before finally colliding with one of the older ewes, half of her tiny body disappearing into the massive fleece. The ewe glanced casually over her shoulder, then went on placidly chewing her hay. Rambling Rose extricated herself from the wooly encounter and wobbled off in search of her mother.

As the weeks passed, Rose developed a regular habit of poking her head deep into the fleeces of the other sheep. At first we thought it was purely accidental, but after a while we recognized it for what it really was—her signature move, her regular calling card. We watched as Rose practiced and perfected this unusual method of identifying her fellow flock members. Most sheep recognize each other through sight or scent, but Rambling Rose settled for nothing so common. With a flourish all her own, she buried her entire head in the fleece of whomever she encountered to determine if it was a friend, a relative, or just a passing acquaintance. Some of the sheep tolerated or simply ignored the indignity, while others took offense and butted Rose away with much grumbling and stamping of feet.

We released most of the lambs from their pens before they were a week old. By that age they were strong enough to hold their own without being trampled by the older sheep, and they were ready to face the outdoor elements. Their mothers, yearning for freedom, grew restless, too. But we kept Rosie and her twins penned for over three weeks. Rambling Rose was totally blind, and we feared for her safety if she were turned loose in the pasture. Finally, as the new grass sprouted and the weather warmed, we could keep them confined no longer. When the three were released, Rosie and her ram lamb shot out the shed door and dashed into the sheep yard, kicking up their heels, reveling in their newfound freedom. Left behind in the dust, Rambling Rose roamed the shed in confusion. She held her head at an angle, listening for her mother. Gradually she worked her way to the door and cautiously stepped out in search of the thoughtless Rosie.

As luck would have it, Rosie already wore a bell. On a trip to Norway years earlier, we had visited some sheep and goat farms in the mountains. The shepherds there told us that a flock's natural leader, its most dominant member, is usually fitted with a bell around her neck. That way the shepherd can more easily locate the sheep when they wander up into the foothills where low-hanging clouds obscure them from view. We liked the idea, and we bought our own sheep bell at a store that was Norway's equivalent of Fleet Farm.

Rosie was unquestionably the most dominant member of our flock, and we ceremoniously belled her when we returned home from Norway. Having the ever-clanging nuisance around her neck didn't improve Rosie's already nasty temper, but we were pleased by the timbre of the sheep bell as we went about our work on the farm.

Rambling Rose's hearing became finely attuned to the sound of her mother's bell. This system worked well when Rosie was awake and moving about the pasture or shed. But her daughter was completely lost when Rosie fell asleep and the sound of the bell was stilled.

I carefully avoided the subject myself, and I was surprised when Terry didn't insist on having Rambling Rose put down as soon as he discovered her blindness. Both Terry and I hate having animals destroyed, and we try to find alternatives whenever possible. But even I must admit that it may be kinder to put down a very sick, distressed, or debilitated animal rather than letting it suffer. I wondered how long Rambling Rose would be with us.

Ragnar and Mrs. Harris

hough lambing season is one of the most fun and exciting times of the year, it also has its moments of extreme exhaustion and disappointment. Even with a small flock, lambing is synonymous with long hours and interrupted sleep. You can count on at least a few obstetric emergencies, and only rarely do all the lambs survive their first few days on earth. It's always a relief when May begins and lambing is over.

Rosie was the last ewe to lamb that spring, and we were able to relax a bit and turn our attention to other matters following the birth of her twins. Terry and I had been thinking about adding another ram to our flock, and Mary had found a nice prospect. At a craft fair, she had met a breeder of purebred Icelandic sheep who was selling a young black ram named Ragnar. We agreed to buy Ragnar in partnership with Mary, thinking he would make a nice complement to Lloyd, our white Shetland ram. Icelandic sheep produce a high-quality spinning fleece, and I looked forward to getting my hands on Ragnar's glossy black wool. While we would continue to breed our purebred Shetland ewes to Lloyd, the new Icelandic ram would be an ideal mate for our Icelandic cross ewes.

One morning in early May, Mary arrived in her pickup truck, towing Ragnar in a livestock trailer. We unloaded him directly through a gate into the sheep yard, where Lloyd and the ewes were watching with interest. At that time of year, all of the ewes and both rams could be kept together in the same pasture. Sheep are photosensitive, meaning their reproductive activity is regulated by length of daylight. The ewes would not be fertile until fall, when the days grew shorter. And until the ewes were in heat, the rams wouldn't fight or become territorial.

Now Ragnar greeted the ewes with enthusiasm. He skipped and pranced throughout the sheep yard while the ewes watched him warily. This was not the man of their dreams, and they wanted nothing to do with him.

Ragnar was young and playful. He was curious, and he had no fear of people. If Terry was repairing a fence, Ragnar was right there beside him, breathing down his neck and bending over his shoulder to see what was going on.

Lloyd's and Ragnar's personalities were as different as the hues of their fleeces. On Lloyd's home farm on the Canadian border, each Shetland ram was named for a British prime minister. Like his namesake, Lloyd was the soul of tact and diplomacy. He didn't cavort around the sheep yard as Ragnar did, tormenting others with his juvenile antics. Lloyd's behavior toward humans and other sheep was respectful and appropriate. He often lay calmly on the grass with a benign look on his face, while his young offspring ran playfully round and round him. The lambs even jumped over Lloyd's back in their more lively games, as he looked on, unconcerned.

Ragnar would never put up with that. In fact, he was more likely to join in the game himself, jumping over Lloyd's prone

form, too. Ragnar teased the ewes and lambs. He even sometimes produced a *hee-haw* sound, as if laughing at the misfor-
tunes of his pasture-mates.

If Ragnar were human he could have enjoyed a successful career in the theater. He could play the villain, the clown,
or the stooge, but never the good guy in the white hat. Ragnar was always the perpetrator—never the victim—of whatever misdeeds occurred in the shed or pasture. His mercurial
temperament kept everyone on their toes.

A good test of the rams' characters occurred one day when
the sheep were caught outside in a hailstorm. Icy marbles
pelted down from the heavens, and the flock thundered home
to the shed. As the galloping herd reached the shed door,
Lloyd stood aside, allowing the ewes and lambs to dash one
by one through the narrow opening ahead of him. Ragnar,
though, reacted differently. He used his impressive curling
horns to jostle his way to the front of the line, heedless of the
cries of the ewes and lambs.

Ragnar wasn't exactly mean; he was just overly playful and
high-spirited.

Because of Ragnar, the morning chore of letting the flock
out of the shed turned into an armed ordeal. Of course, it had
never been simple: first I had to cross through the long shed
bursting with bleating creatures eager to go outside, then
struggle to push open the heavy, dilapidated door to the pasture. Now Ragnar entered the picture. After weeks of fending
off his playful advances when I stepped into the shed each
morning, I learned to carry a weapon of self-defense. I kept
a broken broom handle at the ready whenever Ragnar was
near. Of course, he saw this as a further invitation to play. As
soon as I stepped into the shed, Ragnar rushed at me with his
head down and his massive horns at the forefront. I worked
my way through the flock, fending him off. As I backed toward
the pasture door I often had to whack him across the horns

with my broom handle, scolding him loudly with each step. Some days I felt I had more in common with a prehistoric cavewoman battling a wooly mammoth than I did with most of my office-bound acquaintances.

❊

One day I took a phone call from the administrator of the nearby West Central school district, asking if I could write a grant application for a project: a comprehensive after-school program including music and theater, fitness and recreational activities, and supervised study and tutoring opportunities. A sizeable grant would be needed to make this project happen, but the district had found a potential source: a grant program sponsored by the federal department of education. If received, the grant would make a real impact on the ability of the small rural district's ability to provide extracurricular services to its students.

Because of budget cuts and declining enrollment, rural Minnesota schools were struggling financially. They could provide the basics, but money was scarce for extracurricular activities, sports, and other programs that are available in more populated areas. Although the federal grant program was very competitive, the administrators felt it was worth a try.

We had held a few preliminary meetings, and a plan began to take shape. But it would be a challenge. As with most government grant programs, this one sought to address a specific problem—in this case, to serve "at-risk youth" by helping prevent risky behaviors such as gang-related violence. This angle made the program more relevant in urban settings. How could I develop the proposal in a way that would show the funds were just as desperately needed in rural areas?

I spent hours doing research at the office, aided by Mr. Tinkles, who dozed on the card table guarding the dictionary. The key to success with this application, according to the program guide, was to identify these at-risk behaviors and propose solutions. Statistics show that rural Minnesota teens are far more likely to die as a result of car accidents, and their families have far lower incomes and less access to health care than their urban counterparts. Though important, none of these findings fit the cause-and-effect rationale, explaining how after-school programs would reduce or eliminate the risk factors.

As a part of the grant application process, we surveyed the students in the West Central district to determine their interest in various after-school activities. As we studied the responses, a pattern began to emerge. Though the inner cities had problems with gangs and violence, our children had a totally different reason to need after-school and summer enrichment programs: their geographic isolation.

The Minneapolis school district serves over 35,000 students, but geographically it encompasses less than sixty square miles. The 500-square-mile West Central school district serves just over 800 students. In urban school districts, there are often over 600 students per square mile, but in the West Central district, there are fewer than two. Transportation is a huge issue in this sparsely populated area. On our survey, students were asked if they would participate in after-school or summer activities if such programs were available. Leafing through the individual surveys, it struck me as incredibly sad to read—over and over again—the same reply earnestly penciled in neat cursive writing. To the question, "Do you (or would you) participate in summer recreation programs?" nearly three-quarters of sixth graders answered, "I would really like to, but I can't get a ride."

These children were so sincere and bright and eager— eager to learn and eager to participate. But since they lived twenty or thirty miles from the school, there were few opportunities. Though this was a significant finding, I knew that, as a risk factor, geographic isolation would not rank with gang violence in the minds of application reviewers. Cost-effectiveness was another issue. The cost to transport a relatively small number of children scattered over five hundred square miles would be extremely high on the cost-per-participant calculation.

During the weeks spent researching and writing the grant application, I traveled to the town of Barrett often to meet with the team of administrators and school staff who were on the grant committee. A group of us planned to drive to Moorhead for an applicant training session with a department of education representative, an expert on at-risk youth. Working out of the Chicago office, Mrs. Harris was touring the Midwest, meeting with grant seekers to provide technical assistance. We scheduled an individual meeting with her following the general session. Our application was a long shot, and I knew our assertion that geographic isolation was as important a risk factor as gang-related violence might not go over well with this influential woman.

On the morning of the training session, I got up early and spent an hour in the office, preparing my notes and research materials for the meeting. In my preoccupation I forgot to wake Chris for school, and he nearly missed his bus. Distracted by the rushed morning, I looked at my watch and was shocked to see it was nearly time for me to leave. I packed up my notes and dashed out to the car.

Halfway down the driveway, I noticed the emptiness of the vast pasture, and I remembered. The sheep! I had forgotten to let the sheep out of the shed. Not wanting to waste time changing clothes, I raced back up the driveway, parked the car, and ran to the shed. I glanced down at my clean shoes and tidy office clothes and prayed that Ragnar would not be in a playful mood.

The sheep were milling around inside the shed, agitated

and upset at being forgotten. When they saw me enter, they all jockeyed for position near the big door leading outside to the pasture. I spotted Ragnar near the far wall, and I hoped he would keep his distance while I navigated through the wall-to-wall crush of bodies blocking the path to the door.

I should have known better. When Ragnar caught sight of me, he forced his way toward me through the throng. His dancing eyes and lively step were a dead giveaway. He was in especially high spirits. Despite my meeting in Moorhead, Ragnar would not allow himself to be cheated out of his morning's entertainment.

Grasping the broom handle, I readied myself for another savage clash with the ram. I held my weapon high, facing my opponent. He advanced steadily as I backed toward the shed door. Ragnar lunged, and I responded with a loud yell and a sharp crack of the broom handle across his horns. In this manner we made our way across the shed toward the door.

Maybe it was the delay that morning, or maybe it was the phase of the moon or the alignment of the planets, but whatever the reason, Ragnar was behaving particularly badly. Before I was halfway across the shed, I had several nasty bruises where Ragnar's horned head had met soft flesh.

I increased the volume of my cavewoman yells and beat him over the head and shoulders with the broom handle. Ragnar was unfazed. At one point he had me pinned against the shed wall, where he delivered some agonizing blows. I pummeled his head with a series of thumps that would have left any reasonable living thing in a coma. Ragnar merely paused to shake his head, but it allowed me to sidle my way to the door.

But now I had to lay down my weapon and use both hands to unfasten the baler twine that served as a lock, then push open the heavy door. As I fumbled frantically, Ragnar backed up and readied himself for a massive assault. I sidestepped at just the right moment, and his bony head crashed into the door. The force of his attack worked as a battering ram, and the door swung open. Ragnar scampered outside into the yard, and the battle for the day was done.

My shoes were ruined and my clothes were nearly in shreds. Large purple bruises were already appearing on my arms and legs. I returned to the house, took a quick shower, dressed in clean clothes, and limped out to the car. I hoped I hadn't lost my voice entirely from all the yelling.

The others on the grant committee were waiting when I arrived in Barrett, where we met to ride together to the training session in Moorhead. Throughout the two-hour ride, I shifted uncomfortably in my seat. I felt bruised everywhere, and I tried to keep my hands out of sight. They were still seeping blood.

When the training session was over, we gathered in a small conference room to meet with the representative from the funding source. As we introduced ourselves, Mrs. Harris, the influential woman from Chicago, smiled warmly. She squeezed my hand and said, "It's wonderful to meet you."

I winced at the firm handshake. "I'm pleased to meet you, too," I said, hoping Mrs. Harris hadn't noticed my skinned knuckles.

We discussed our project and explained why we believed our population of rural youth was as deserving of federal funding as were the multiracial gangs of the inner city.

I don't think Mrs. Harris agreed completely with our philosophy, but her comments were gracious and kind. She said, "You raise some excellent points, though I'm afraid the funding source is looking more for projects that address at-risk behaviors in terms of actual *violence*." As she spoke, she folded her reading glasses, gathered her notes, and began to pack her briefcase. She continued, "But anyway, I'm so glad to see your dedication and zeal for the cause. I really believe we could eradicate all violence in society if everyone were as dedicated and peace-loving as you people are."

It felt strange to be sitting around a table in such a civilized manner—calmly discussing strategies to prevent violence and risky behaviors—when my voice was still hoarse from the battle cry and my knuckles bruised and bleeding after mercilessly beating an animal over the head with a blunt object. I said nothing to the others about my encounter in the sheep shed. It somehow seemed inappropriate.

The meeting was over. Mrs. Harris returned to Chicago, and we drove back to Barrett. Despite the odds, we submitted our grant application. It was not successful. The funding went to several inner-city projects on the East Coast, and no doubt the money was well spent. But I couldn't help thinking of the West Central students who so earnestly filled out those surveys. There would be no enrichment opportunities for the eager young learners this time around.

Our committee held a debriefing meeting at the district office shortly after we received the rejection. I felt terribly guilty at failing my clients, but like true Scandinavian Americans, the grant committee members bore their disappointment stoically.

"Well, it could be worse," said the chairman.

"Ya," added another member in her Scandinavian brogue. "At least we don't have any of those gangs around here."

I nodded my head in agreement. But still, I thought to myself as I massaged my scabby knuckles, not even a woman as wise and urbane as Mrs. Harris can convince me that violence occurs only in the city.

Shearing

I t was the first week of May, and the sheep hadn't been sheared. We'd had weeks of cold, wet weather in April, and flocks that wintered outside would be unshearable until they dried out. The shearer had a month-long backlog. Finally we had reached the top of his list, and he would be coming today.

In the morning, Terry and I hurried from house to shed and from outbuilding to outbuilding, gathering all the necessary equipment and supplies. The sheep were already confined in the small yard just outside the shed. The older ones knew something was up. They milled around the pen, jumpy and agitated. The lambs picked up on their mothers' anxiety, and they galloped skittishly around the yard.

Jim the shearer came down from Otter Tail County. Our area had few professional shearers, and it was hard to find one who would travel any distance unless he could be guaranteed about fifty animals to shear, since he would be paid by the head. We worked together with some other small flock owners to lure Jim to our farm each spring. Mary—along with some weekend shepherds who kept a few sheep each— brought their animals to our place for shearing, so Jim would have a respectable quantity of sheep when he arrived.

Before Jim got there, Terry and I penned the rams and ewes in the shed, while the lambs were sent out to the pasture. The lambs didn't go far. They gathered at the closed gate to the sheep yard, bleating dramatically for their mothers. Meanwhile, their mothers kept up an ear-splitting din inside the shed, calling to their lambs.

Mary arrived, towing her eight sheep in a livestock trailer, and after Mary came Jim. Seemingly deaf to the commotion, Jim set up shop in the south half of the shed. He scattered old canvas tarps over the floor to keep the straw bedding from mixing with the wool. Then he lay down a sheet of plywood to create a flat, even work surface. Jim hung the motor of his electric shearing rig from a rope flung over a rafter in the shed, and he was ready to go.

Jim's face was lit with its usual boyish grin and was topped by a shock of gravity-defying white hair. He picked up his shears, waggled his eyebrows, and said to the ewes in a convincing Groucho Marx impersonation, "Well, ladies, who's first?"

Jim was a fast and experienced shearer, and he kept up an ongoing monologue as he separated the nervous ewes from their fleeces. His fee varied from three to ten dollars a head, depending on the price of gas and a host of other mysterious variables.

When Jim sheared a sheep, it looked as effortless as a knife cutting through warm butter. The wool seemed to melt off the sheep as he worked, from head to tail, then across the flanks, and finally down the belly and legs. He averaged less than five minutes a sheep. Terry caught and dragged the unwilling victims over to Jim's tarp-covered shearing platform, and then he flipped them for Jim. No matter how hard they struggled in Terry's grip, once they were flipped onto their rumps, sitting straight up, the sheep sat placidly until the shearing was done.

Shearing looks easy when done by a professional, but in reality it is a backbreaking job. Standing the whole time, the shearer bends over the sheep, often for hours at a stretch. When we kept only eight sheep, Terry sheared them himself with hand shears. Two sheep each evening after work was enough: for days afterward he suffered agonizing backaches.

While Jim worked, Mary and I skirted the shorn fleeces on a big plywood rectangle balanced on sawhorses. Skirting is the removal of the dirty, unusable parts of the fleece—mostly the wool clipped from the belly, legs, and rear. We threw the skirtings into a pile to be used as garden mulch.

Jim was an expert on all sorts of topics. He was a farmer and shepherd himself, and he had acquired wisdom far beyond his years as he traveled from farm to farm shearing sheep. In addition to his impressive knowledge of world affairs, local politics, and the weather, Jim could guess the age of any animal as he was shearing it.

"This one's four," he would say as he bent over a ewe. Or "This one's about two and a half. Am I correct?"

Like the Amazing Kreskin in overalls, Jim seemed almost psychic. He could tell which ewes had been pregnant over the winter just by the volume and luster of their fleeces. Using the same method, he could guess who was raising twins and who had borne only a single lamb. Jim remembered particular members of our flock from year to year, even though he had sheared thousands of sheep since then.

While shearing Rosie, Jim looked up and said, "This lady's getting a little long in the tooth. Maybe it's time to give the butcher a call." He grinned at me, knowing his remark would get a reaction. Sheep start to lose some teeth by the age of five or six. Without a full set of teeth, they can't chew very effectively, and the condition and volume of their fleece declines due to the lack of nutrition. Both Rosie and Ada turned five that summer, and we had noticed a decrease in wool production. Still, Jim knew that this operation ran partly on sentiment.

Four hours later, the shearing was done, and the sheep were released from the shed. Terry went to the pasture gate to let the lambs back into the yard. As he pulled the gate open, the lambs, feeling hugely neglected and put out, streamed into the yard in search of their mothers.

Mary pointed to one of the small forms darting through the crush of bodies and said, "That's a really nice-looking ram lamb. You ought to think of selling him for breeding." That was Buck, Rambling Rose's twin. Unlike his undersized and delicate sister, Buck was developing into a robust, strapping specimen of Shetland manhood. Terry and I had talked about his potential as a breeding ram a few times already, and we both felt he was shaping up well. One of the items at the top of my shepherdess to-do list was to place an ad for Buck in a nationally distributed sheep breeders' magazine.

The ewes weren't accustomed to their new spring haircuts, and they stepped cautiously around the yard. They didn't recognize each other after the shearing, and skirmishes broke out everywhere. One ewe roughly head butted someone she took to be a perfect stranger but who had been her best friend yesterday. Even the lambs didn't recognize their mothers without their familiar fleeces. These naked ewes looked and smelled different, and the lambs ran right past them in search of their real mothers.

If the post-shearing fights got too rough, we penned the sheep together in a very small space until they got used to each other all over again. If sheep can't back up far enough to get a good run at each other, they won't fight. It's a nearly foolproof method of ensuring a new member of the flock won't get beat up, and it's a trick that is used to keep rams from bashing their heads together. One overnight is enough: by morning they've usually forgotten what they were mad about.

Though shearing is hard and dirty work, the pleasant company made it a fun, festive day. When the work was done we sprawled out across the grass, easing our aching backs, arms, and legs, clothes stiff with greasy lanolin, manure, and a few random spatters of blood. Rosie and Ada stood just on the other side of the yard fence, eyeing the collection of humans stretched on the lawn. Rosie watched Jim, in particular. Rosie was no fool, and she was keeping her guard up, just in case he should attack what was left of her fleece.

Half an hour later, the men rose to their feet, and Jim started to gather his shearing equipment. He and Terry retrieved the motor, plywood, and tarps from the shed and loaded them into the back of Jim's truck. Jim wiped the worst of the grime from his hands with a greasy rag, then he leaned over the sheep's watering trough.

"Better get rid of them old ewes," he advised again, as he sluiced his head and arms with cool water from the trough. "You can't make a living off their looks."

Rosie glared at Jim, as if she understood every word he said.

"But I like the old ewes." I said. "They've got a lot of personality."

"You can't take that to the bank," said Jim before he tossed the last of his equipment into the truck and drove away.

Terry began carrying the bags of wool away to the machine shed loft. Mary and I were in no hurry to leave our shady spot, and as we sat resting on the grass, I told Mary about Terry's ultimatum.

"I've got to start making a profit with the animals, or we're going to have to sell most of them," I told her.

"Well, the first thing you have to realize it that you can't run an old folks' home for sheep," she said. We both laughed.

Mary had become a mentor in my transition from hobby farmer to serious shepherdess. She and her husband ran an organic dairy along with raising horses, hogs, sheep, and chickens on a small, hilly piece of land. Mary and her husband are well-educated, intelligent people who have chosen a life that is rich in its simplicity. They raised their family on an income that might have been meager at times, but it allowed them the freedom to pursue meaningful, rewarding lives. Aside from occasional outside jobs, they earned their entire income from their small farm and the sale of Mary's woven rugs. Farming wasn't their hobby, it was their livelihood.

"But seriously," said Mary, "There's not much room for sentiment if you're going to make it in farming. When an animal isn't producing any longer, you've got to get rid of it."

We sat in silence for a few minutes while I considered Mary's advice. Rosie and Ada were nearing the end of their productive years, but I didn't think I could ever bear to sell either of them. Not only did these types of decisions cost us money, my weakness for collecting odd and amusing animals could also bring down the quality of the flock. Mary's advice was sound but would be hard to accept.

I walked Mary to her truck and climbed up to look in on the eight naked-looking sheep in the trailer. They were only half the size of their pre-shorn selves, and the trailer that had been nearly bursting at the seams with sheep that morning now looked half empty.

"Where's Spot?" I asked. "I didn't see her here today." I knew and recognized most of Mary's sheep. Spot, a regular at our annual shearing event and a particular favorite of Mary's, was missing.

"In the freezer," said Mary. "We made her into sausage last winter."

Egg-sucking dog

The four dogs were an integral part of our life on the farm. Bart and Petey were sheepdogs. We had big plans to train them to work sheep, but their skills stayed at a very basic level. There was no doubt the dogs had the herding instinct, though. When they chased my car down the driveway, Bart and Petey used a classic tandem side-to-side sweeping formation. They had all the moves of skilled and seasoned sheepdogs.

Petey was the natural leader, and she carved a bold arc to the right of the speeding vehicle. Bart took the left flank, and together they herded the car down the driveway. Once the car's tires crunched to a halt at the end of the gravel path and turned onto the county road, the dogs considered their duty done. They turned around and loped back to the farm.

Petey and Bart also used these handy techniques with other species, such as cats and small children. They perceived any two- or four-legged moving object as something that needed to be herded from point A to point B.

※

Keeyla and Karsey (known as "the girls") were Beth's dogs. When Beth moved from a house to an apartment in Minneapolis, she dropped the girls off at our farm. "It's just temporary," she said, "just until I can find a place where I can keep pets." Two years later, the girls were still with us, and there was no indication things were going to change anytime soon.

Keeyla and Karsey were city dogs, accustomed to regular baths, grooming appointments, and restful indoor living. Then they found themselves relocated to the country, where bathing was optional and no self-respecting dog ever had her hair or nails done. In no time at all, the once chic and stylish pair had reverted back to nature.

Karsey was the result of an unlikely mating between a German shorthaired pointer and a miniature dachshund. She had the color and general appearance of a very large standard dachshund. But, if you got a closer look at her, it was clear that something had gone seriously wrong in the gene pool. Karsey's ears hung nearly to the ground, and her short, stubby legs were massive. Her feet turned out at an angle, and when she walked, her long, thick midsection swayed from side to side. Because of her misshapen head and snout, Karsey's baggy lips were perpetually caught up on some of her teeth. She looked like a gargoyle or a very ugly garden gnome.

Karsey had only one saving grace. She kept our property free of salespeople. It didn't matter that she was gentle by nature and terrified of strangers. She looked ferocious to anyone who drove into the yard, because her long yellow teeth were nearly always exposed. People didn't dare to get out of their cars after they'd seen Karsey.

Keeyla, unfailingly cheerful and energetic, was a black chow chow. Life for Keeyla was one long smorgasbord of experiences to sample and savor. She greeted every person and animal she encountered with excitement, curiosity, and enthusiasm. That was simply her nature, the way herding cars and cats and flocks of wild geese came instinctively to Bart and Petey.

To keep Keeyla from roaming and to protect all four dogs from coyotes, skunks, and other nocturnal hazards, they spent their nights together in a fenced kennel in the back yard. Inside the kennel was a three-room doghouse, the Casa de Pero, a long, sprawling affair. At one end was a big, well-insulated room. Next to that was a slightly smaller compartment, and finally, at the far end, was a tiny porchlike space. When the dogs were on speaking terms, all four of them slept together in the big room. That section of the Casa was painted red and plastered with bumper stickers that screamed *Liberate the Captives!* and *Free Tibet!*

When the four dogs got into one of their frequent fracases in the kennel, sides were chosen. Always, it was the girls versus the sheepdogs. With their big-city wiles and feminine cunning, the girls came out on top, and they claimed the big room for themselves. The more submissive sheepdogs sought shelter in the smaller and less comfortable cubbyholes when the big house was under siege by the girls.

The dogs' basic routine didn't vary much from day to day. When the weather was hot, the dogs slept in the shade. When the weather was cold, the dogs slept in the sun. They devoted at least twenty of the day's twenty-four hours to sleeping. And though they got plenty of shut-eye, the experience never looked particularly restful. Their sleep was fitful—lips twitching, legs thrashing, eyelids blinking—clearly in nightmarish pursuit of squirrels, rabbits, and in Keeyla's case, Black Betty the goat. But they were apparently well rested enough, because in the few waking hours remaining, they were raring to go.

Bart, Petey, and Karsey never left the farm. They seemed to have an innate understanding of where the property lines ran and the importance of staying at home. Keeyla, on the other hand, had no such inhibitions. Unless she was closely supervised, she tended to wander. Though she never went far and had never gotten herself into any trouble, we had to work at keeping Keeyla at home.

Chris's main responsibility that year was the care, feeding, and supervision of the four dogs—a surprisingly complicated job. But since Chris was in school until early June, Keeyla-watching duty fell to me during the daytime. As long as someone was outside with her, Keeyla stayed nearby, and she never bothered our animals. Her first two years with us were uneventful. Then one day Black Betty appeared in the distant meadow, and everything changed.

Our neighbor Abe got Black Betty the goat that spring, and soon Betty gave birth to twin kids. Black Betty and her kids spent their days staked out in a meadow that was visible from our yard, about a quarter mile away. Keeyla spent most of her waking hours that spring and summer obsessing about Black Betty and her kids.

Country dwellers who keep small livestock or free range poultry are understandably paranoid about roaming dogs. As a neighborly courtesy, we shoot each other's dogs with BB guns whenever they show up on our property. It works like a local vigilante committee, and it's very effective. Many times that spring and summer I called Abe's mother. "Hey, Bonnie, would you go out and shoot that black dog that's running with the goats?" I had a good view of the goat grazing meadow from my kitchen window, and often I could see Keeyla romping there.

Whenever Bonnie's children had a new dog, we got similar phone calls: "Would you run out and shoot that yellow dog that's coming across?"

When someone in the neighborhood gets a new dog, there is a tacit grace period. The neighbors are warned about the new dog, and its owner assumes the dog will be shot only with

BB guns during that time. We all hope the new dog quickly develops an aversion to calling on the neighbors. Because once a dog kills a chicken or gets a taste of sheep's blood, it can't be stopped. And then the dog gets shot for real.

Keeyla's grace period was running out. Though she had never harmed the goats, she was making far too many social calls on Black Betty's turf. The sting of BBs didn't curb Keeyla's enthusiasm. To make matters worse, neighbors to the west and north were also reporting Keeyla sightings in their yards.

One morning I looked out the kitchen window, and there was Keeyla again running with Betty and the goat kids. I tried calling Bonnie, but there was no answer. I decided to go after Keeyla. Overland, the quarter-mile walk to the goat pasture would entail crossing three fences and a slough. The quickest way to stop Keeyla would be to take a two-mile drive.

I got in the car and drove over to Bonnie's. Keeyla liked to ride in the car, and she forgot all about Black Betty when I opened the passenger door for her. Once I had her in the car, she was a captive audience, and I figured I'd have another heart-to-heart talk with her.

I said, "Keeyla, you've got to stop chasing goats! One of these days you're going to get into real trouble. You've got to learn!" Keeyla simply smiled up at me, dancing across the seat, wagging her entire body, licking my face. It was no use trying to reason with her.

As we neared our farm we met Leroy, a retired farmer who lived just down the road. I turned into our driveway, and Leroy pulled up behind me. I waited a long while for him to climb out of his ancient pickup and mosey up to lean into my open car window. Leroy rested his forearm along the top of the car door, and he took his time adjusting the wad of chewing tobacco that bulged out his lower lip.

"You gonna have any hay to sell this summer?" he asked.

"I doubt it. We're hoping to keep back some more ewe lambs this year, and we don't want to run short," I said. "I can ask Terry, though. See what he thinks."

"Halvorson's looking for some horse hay. Told him I'd ask around." Leroy reached out a gnarled hand to pat Keeyla's head. She danced with excitement at the attention. She stood on my lap, her head out the window, wagging and wiggling all over, smiling up at Leroy.

Leroy seemed in no hurry to move on, so I told him about the trouble Keeyla was causing. After telling him the whole long story, I said, "I just don't know what to do with her. Either she's chasing goats or running all over the neighborhood. I'm just about at the end of my rope with this dog."

Leroy leaned away from the car and spat a long stream of tobacco juice into the ditch. He thought for a time, adjusting his cap, running a hand over his stubbly chin, scratching the back of his leathery neck, squinting up at the sky. It was a long while before he spoke.

"What you got yourself there is a regular ol' egg-suckin' dog," said Leroy. "She ain't gonna learn. You can't do nothin' about it. Best to shoot her sooner rather than later."

Keeyla wiggled her whole body in excitement, waving her black bushy tail, darting her head in and out of the car window, trying to lick Leroy's face, begging him to pet her again.

Leroy gave Keeyla one last scratch behind the ears. He said, "Let me know about that hay." Then he ambled back to his pickup and reversed slowly out onto the highway.

I drove the rest of the way home and parked the car in the garage. I turned to look at the sleek black dog sitting beside me. Cheerful, friendly, healthy, happy, beautiful. A great dog, really. If only it weren't for all of those bad habits.

Like a scarlet letter, the label *egg-suckin' dog* carried a stigma in the farm community. It's what the old timers called a dog that was shiftless and good-for-nothing, sucking the marrow out of the very thing it was supposed to protect. Keeyla had been marked.

❊

As a child, I was fascinated by the story of another egg-sucking dog. Before I was old enough for school, I went to Garfield with my dad almost every day. We went right after the morning milking, hauling a truckload of ten-gallon milk cans to the creamery. While we waited for the cans to be emptied, we'd go to the café. At that time of day the café was packed with farmers, still in their barn pants and boots, all killing half an hour waiting for their milk cans to be emptied.

We squeezed into a booth with some of Dad's buddies. There were usually seven of us wedged tight into a booth— three men on one side, and three men and me on the other. When Dad and I got there, one of the guys yelled to the waitress, "Bring over another cup of coffee and a bottle of that orange pop."

Conversation lapsed into the usual topics. They talked about the Twins, the weather, and the price of corn. Every once in a while they would get onto the subject of animals. They were all farmers, and they had some great stories. Hogs that saved human lives. A sheepdog that raised a litter of kittens after the mother cat had been run over by a tractor.

During a lull in the conversation, I'd pipe up and say to Don, the storyteller, "Tell about the time Earl brought that fancy coonhound up from Louisiana on the train." Or my favorite: "Tell about that egg-sucking dog."

Don's booming laugh would echo in the high-sided booth, and if I was lucky, he'd tell the story.

"You mean that egg-suckin' dog that Bob shot in the head with a .22? Okay, I'll tell it. You remember how Harriet just got fed up with that dog suckin' eggs in the henhouse all the time? She'd been after Bob to shoot that dog for months. So, finally, one day Bob took him in the pickup and drove out into the alfalfa—you know that forty he's got west of the machine shed? He took him out there so the kids wouldn't see.

"Bob told the dog to sit, not five yards away. And the damn thing just sat right there, lookin' Bob square in the eye. Bob took aim and shot just once. The bullet bounced clean off that dog's skull. Didn't hardly stun him. Left just a little nick in the hide of his forehead.

"Bob took it as a sign from God. The dog was still sittin' there, so Bob went and hung his gun on the rack in the pickup. Then he held the door wide open so the dog could climb in. The dog was still a little shell-shocked, so Bob had to help him up.

"Bob brought that dog back home, just like nothin' had happened. Harriet couldn't get over it that Bob shot him just the once. But he wouldn't shoot him again, no matter what Harriet said. The dog died of old age about ten years later. Always had a nice pelt on him, though, from suckin' all them eggs."

The waitress came around to top up the coffee cups. "Quit with the stories, Don," she said. "You're gonna scare the kid." She used her free hand to ruffle up my hair. With a wink and a smile she'd say to me, "You need to find yourself another table to sit at, girl. Find yourself some decent company."

Before long, one of the guys would look at his watch and say, "Them cans should be out by now." The men would gulp down their coffee, throw some change on the table, and tromp back out to their pickups.

The next morning we'd be back in the same booth at the café. There would be more talk about the Twins, the weather, and the price of beans. The waitress would pour coffee, ruffle my hair, and trade insults with the men. Then there'd be a lull in the conversation, and I'd say to Don, "Would you tell again about that egg-sucking dog?"

Summer vacation

As the first of June approached, both the flock and the family were enjoying the soft, spring weather. The lambs romped in the sun while their mothers grazed. The pasture was greening up, and the ewes spent entire days intently cropping mouthful after mouthful of the lush green grass. The nursing lambs took a heavy toll on the ewes, and the ewes needed to graze steadily throughout the daylight hours if they were to nourish both themselves and their lambs.

The first of June signaled another major milestone. School was out for the summer. Much as I enjoyed Chris's company, his presence at the office during the summer months created some complications.

I really tried to maintain a professional image when working with my clients, especially during those first months of starting my consulting business. Whenever I met with my clients, I traveled to their offices—mostly city and county governments and nonprofit agencies throughout western Minnesota. I didn't think my clients would consider me a serious, legitimate consultant unless they could visualize me in a well-organized office setting, surrounded by state-of-the-art technology. *Not* sitting at a card table, on a bent three-legged folding chair, in a cat-infested living room, in the middle of a sheep farm.

Chris did little to further my professional image. At the sound of the telephone's ring, he would try to beat me to it, answering with a deep "You rang?" in his best imitation of Lurch from *The Addams Family*.

Once school was out, Chris and his friends kept up a noisy clamor both inside and outside the house. It was hard for me to concentrate on work. But, I kept reminding myself, being at home with Chris was one of the most important benefits of the consulting work, especially during the summer when he was home all day. I tried to keep my complaints to a minimum.

Chris was an easygoing kid with a great sense of humor. Despite his laid-back nature, he had one all-consuming passion, one that became an obsession by the time he was twelve. His obsession took various guises, all of which had one object in common—to launch his small form into thin air while mounted upon some type of wheeled contraption. Skateboards and bicycles were his first mediums of self-destruction. Later came dirt bikes and other motorized vehicles.

Every winter, Chris saved his weekly allowance. When summer came, he went to Menards or Fleet Farm and bought angle iron, two-by-four lumber, and huge sheets of plywood. He spent most of his summer vacation in the garage and machine shed, busily sawing, hammering, and eventually even welding, in his quest to build mammoth platforms and ramps from which to hurl himself. Chris often had one or two friends over at our house helping with his projects. My days in the office were punctuated by the boys' shouts of delight when their stunts were successful and trips to the hospital emergency room when things didn't go as well.

Terry and I tried to balance out Chris's perilous lifestyle by giving him extra chores. His basic responsibilities were the care, feeding, and supervision of the dogs and the three house cats. Keeping track of Keeyla took up a lot of his time. The cats didn't require much effort on Chris's part, but he liked spending time with them, and they provided some good entertainment.

Though their names implied a union, Mr. and Mrs. Tinkles didn't live in matrimonial harmony. If a marriage did exist, it was strictly one of convenience, since the two cats were forced to share the same food bowl and litter box.

Mrs. Tinkles was a fat, crabby old cat who grew fatter and angrier with each passing year. The short furry pelt that stretched to cover her massive body was a glossy black sprinkled with flecks of orange. She would have been a very pretty animal if she'd lost a few pounds and improved her attitude. Mr. Tinkles was half Siamese and half gray alley cat. Huge and lean, he handled himself with the grace and majesty of a tiger. I suppose it was understandable that he was disappointed in the arranged marriage that saddled him with the neurotic, spiteful old harridan that was Mrs. Tinkles.

Young Luigi, though, was sweet and good. He was playful, happy, and nearly as eager to please as a puppy. Though Luigi did occasionally ambush people from the top of the antique dresser, there really was no malice in him. But Mr. and Mrs. Tinkles were as black-hearted as a couple of cauldron-stirring old witches.

Moreover, Mr. Tinkles had become an absolute menace during mealtimes, insisting on playing the Nerf gun game. He was even worse when we had company over for dinner. For the sake of etiquette, I packed my Nerf gun away when guests arrived. When Mr. Tinkles realized the gun was nowhere in sight, he went wild. While we were dining on special occasions such as Christmas or Thanksgiving, Mr. Tinkles often appeared out of nowhere, streaked across the room, and leapt onto the table, landing on top of the roast turkey or glazed ham.

We learned we could save ourselves a lot of grief if we banished the cats to the basement whenever we invited guests for a meal. But the guests invariably asked about the whereabouts of the three cats, and I felt guilty to admit they were locked in a small concrete bunker in the basement. Our son-in-law, Jeremy, helped to ease my conscience by suggesting we think of a better name for the cats' hideaway. He recommended the Hamptons. So the next Thanksgiving, when our dinner guests arrived and asked, "Where are all those cats?" we could honestly reply, "They've gone to the Hamptons for the holiday."

That summer—when they weren't busy at the office or vacationing in the Hamptons—Mr. and Mrs. Tinkles spent most of their free time relaxing in their very own castle. Years earlier, Chris had gotten a cardboard castle for his birthday, and Terry had set it up in the living room. About three feet square and four feet tall, complete with towers, turrets, and a working drawbridge, the Create-Your-Own-Castle was a real hit. Its white surface was outlined with the classic castle features—crenellations, flags, coats of arms, window boxes—ready to be colored in.

Eventually, as Chris grew older and lost interest in it, the castle was packed up and stored in the basement. But this year, a nostalgic mood struck Chris on one of the first days of his summer vacation. He found the old cardboard castle in the basement, dragged it out, and set it up once more in the living room for old time's sake.

The castle had been assembled and demolished countless times during Chris's early years, and it had become beat-up and shabby. Seen through the jaded eye of a twelve-year-old, the once magical plaything now looked like nothing more than a big, warped, cardboard box. Chris soon lost interest in it again, and it sat abandoned.

Meanwhile, the cats sensed this stately residence had become available. Before long, Mr. and Mrs. Tinkles had taken possession of the castle. Finally, they had found a home worthy of their exalted presences.

The cats were oblivious to the decaying state of their royal manor. The once sturdy cardboard had become bent and droopy. The walls were coming apart at the seams, and the tower leaned at a precarious angle. The turrets were askew, the drawbridge was nearly ripped off, and the entire surface was covered in erratic slashes of vivid color, courtesy of a nap-deprived three-year-old gone wild with a set of permanent markers. The cockeyed fortress could easily have been the brainchild of mad King Ludwig of Bavaria, created in the dementia of his declining years.

The cats were unconcerned with such minor details. Mr. Tinkles proudly assumed his role as lord of the manor with Mrs. Tinkles its disagreeable chatelaine. Poor Luigi was rarely allowed inside the castle, and he could never be more than a lowly serf in this elaborate charade acted out by his companions.

The Tinkleses' castle sat beside my card table desk in the living room. I was relieved to find that the cats preferred to lurk in the castle rather than to sprawl across my card table most of the time.

-*-

Despite having to bear the burden of his disorderly charges, Chris was happy to be out of school. He spent most of his time outside, and his constant companions—in addition to the dogs—were Lamb Chop and Rambling Rose.

Chris took over the bottle-feeding of Lamb Chop and Whiplash in early June. The two lambs were already nibbling grass for much of their diet, but they still loved their feedings. Their twice-a-day bottles were more of a treat than a necessity for the lambs by this time.

Whiplash downed her milk quickly and was ready to return to the pasture and Tony. But Lamb Chop stubbornly refused to go back into the shed or pasture after finishing her bottle, and Chris rarely forced her. She spent most summer days tagging along with Chris and his friends, tailed by the dogs.

When Chris returned Whiplash to the pasture each morning, he usually brought Rambling Rose out with him—rather than leaving her circling aimlessly while her inattentive mother napped or grazed nearby. Chris carried Rose along to wherever his activities would take him that day. Rambling Rose endured rides on Chris's bike and skateboard without complaint, but she didn't enjoy extreme sports participation nearly as much as did Lamb Chop and the dogs. Mostly she loved to cuddle. She could find the perfect crevice under Chris's chin to insert and nuzzle her little face. Rose was completely content when she was held closely in one's arms. She sighed with pleasure and satisfaction at those times, and before long her bronze eyelashes fluttered and closed, and she was asleep.

In the first weeks of Rambling Rose's life, Terry, Chris, and I spent hours tracking down the wandering lamb and returning her to her mother and the lambing pen in the shed. But after all the sheep were turned loose in the pasture, Rose's wanderlust evaporated. She learned quickly that in order to survive, she would need to devote most of her time and attention to keeping up with her mother and remaining within the protective cover of the flock.

Like Chris, I spent as much time as possible outside in June. The spring weather was fantastic, and the animals provided endless entertainment. Tony and Camilla the llama were in high spirits, and they chased the barn cats around the pasture. The young lambs formed a rowdy gang when they were released in the morning. The lamb gang played a wild game of follow-the-leader, running round and round the pasture before jumping off a small dirt cliff, one by one.

Lamb Chop, though, was not happy with her barnyard surroundings. She had no intention of hanging out with a bunch of sheep. She believed she was human. Or if not exactly human, her status was at least equal to that of the dogs.

Lamb Chop became a skilled escape artist and seldom remained long in the pasture or sheep shed. When Chris's friends visited, Lamb Chop felt she should be included in whatever activities were on the agenda. One day the boys took time out from their mega-ramp building project to play a game of baseball. They set up bases and took turns batting. When I looked out the window to see how things were going, I was surprised to see Lamb Chop rounding third base and then crossing home plate.

The boys were delighted when Lamb Chop took an interest in their game. After watching the first inning, she was ready to take a turn. She stood beside the boy who was batting, and when he hit the ball and ran to first base, Lamb Chop followed him. She continued on to second base, then third, and she crossed home plate, touching each of the bases. She repeated this feat several times, but the boys were disappointed to find that Lamb Chop had no intention of taking her turn in the outfield.

A thief in the night

Whiplash, too, was thriving. Like Lamb Chop, Whiplash was curious, outgoing, and loveable. Not to mention clever. One morning when Chris and I went out to the sheep shed to feed Whiplash her morning bottle, we were surprised to see her running cheerfully around the shed, not looking the least bit hungry. She showed no interest in her bottle.

Lambs that nurse from their mothers feed dozens of times a day, whereas bottle lambs usually get their daily nutrition in just three or four large servings. Bottle lambs are always desperately hungry for their morning bottle, and Whiplash's odd behavior had me worried.

I called Terry at work. "You didn't feed Whiplash her morning bottle before you left for work today, did you?"

"No. Why do you ask?" he said.

I explained my concern with her lack of appetite. Terry suggested that I keep an eye on Whiplash to make certain she wasn't coming down with something. As I went about the morning chores, my concern for Whiplash increased. Soon I was imagining her lying in the shed, stricken with some serious illness. But if she was sick, surely she wouldn't have been so energetic, would she?

I was relieved to find, when Chris and I returned for her afternoon feeding, that Whiplash was more than ready for her bottle. She drank it with her usual enthusiasm. But the next morning, she again showed no interest in either Chris or the bottle as she trotted happily around the ewes lying in the shed. This pattern continued for a few days before Terry stumbled upon the answer.

One night Terry and I were awakened at midnight by the sound of barking dogs. During a lull between barking episodes, we could hear the high-pitched yip of coyotes. Our dogs were barking aggressively in response to the coyotes' howl. The dogs were pleading to be let out of their kennel to drive the predators away.

Terry flung off the covers and said, "I'd better go out and check on the sheep. Those coyotes sound awfully close."

Half an hour later, Terry returned and told me what he had discovered. As soon as he stepped out of the house, he could hear clearly the piercing yip of the coyotes. In the cold, crisp night air, their voices carried, and they sounded very near. The dogs vigorously renewed their barking when they heard Terry striding across the yard.

Though the coyotes sounded close, Terry judged their location to be high in the wooded hills at the far corner of the farm. The coyotes were not close enough to threaten the livestock, and much to their disappointment, the dogs were not released. Terry headed for the dark shape of the sheep shed to make sure all of the doors were closed tight and everyone was safe inside.

He pulled open the small side door of the shed and flipped on the light switch. A few of the sheep were startled by this sudden disruption of their night's rest. But, despite the racket of the coyotes and dogs, most of the ewes remained fast asleep. Terry counted the recumbent forms, checking to see that everyone was safely inside.

Though sheep usually sleep on their bellies with all four legs tucked underneath them, ewes with nursing lambs sometimes find it more comfortable to lie slightly on one side, with the full and swollen udder exposed. That is the position in which Terry found most of the dozing ewes that night. They were exhausted from the draining task of feeding their growing lambs, and they slept soundly.

Just as he was ready to turn off the light and return to the house, Terry noticed the small figure of Whiplash sneaking stealthily across the shed floor. She crept up beside a sleeping ewe. Darting a nervous glance at her unsuspecting victim, Whiplash dipped her head and helped herself to a quick drink from the bulging udder. She then sidled on to the next ewe, stealing another swallow of milk. Showing no remorse, Whiplash wore a creamy milk mustache as she made her rounds through the shed, visiting each of the slumbering matrons. The exhausted ewes slept on, cluelessly.

When they are awake, the ewes jealously guard their milk supply, and no one but their own lambs are allowed near the udders. But the old ewes slept soundly in the night, and before long Whiplash grew fat on her stolen bounty.

Lamb kill

Over the next few weeks, Keeyla's obsession with Black Betty grew to epic proportions. She just couldn't seem to leave the goat alone. She had started visiting other farms on a more regular basis, too. After being retrieved from various neighbors' places half a dozen times during the first weeks of June, Keeyla found herself confined to the kennel. If we were working outside in the yard or in the sheep shed, we sometimes let Keeyla out, but only under the strictest supervision.

Scolding, punishing, tying her up—nothing seemed to get the point across to Keeyla that she needed to stay home. Not even serving as target practice for the neighbors taught her anything. Just as Leroy predicted: "She ain't gonna learn."

Before being restricted to the kennel, Keeyla ran, jumped, and rolled through her days with abandon. She made the most of every waking moment. Being confined to the kennel was hard on her.

One Saturday morning, Terry and I were up early to get a head start on the long list of projects that needed to be tackled that day. Terry had gone outside about fifteen minutes ahead of me to start on his work in the shed. It was just getting light when I stepped outside, and I could barely make out the shifting shapes of the lamb gang galloping out toward the far pasture. Terry had just turned the sheep out of the shed.

As usual, the first order of business for me was to let the three dogs out of the kennel. In the dim light it was hard to see which dog was which as they rushed through the gate. I guarded the opening, careful to prevent Keeyla from squeezing out. But before I knew it, all four dogs were through the gate and gone.

I wasn't too concerned about Keeyla's escape. After all, she'd been with us for two years and never really done any harm. Her roaming needed to stop, but I didn't think it was a problem for her to have an hour or two of freedom when both Terry and I were outside. I'd catch her and return her to the kennel well before noon.

About ten minutes later, a torrent of frenzied barking erupted in the pasture. Near the gate leading to the far pasture was Keeyla, yipping, yapping, and running in circles.

Terry stepped out of the shed and met me as I ran to the pasture gate. "Now what?" he said. I hated to admit I'd let Keeyla slip out of the kennel. The other three dogs had been with Terry in the shed, and he knew they weren't the cause of the disturbance.

We reached the spot where Keeyla was raising an almighty ruckus, and there we found one of our youngest lambs. Its throat was ripped wide open, and blood stained the grass around its body.

Terry caught Keeyla roughly and held her down. He pried her jaw open to look in her mouth. A dog that has killed sheep almost always bears the telltale sign of wool stuck in its teeth, and Terry needed to see the evidence. He examined her teeth, and then he ran his finger across her tongue and over the roof of her mouth to check for blood. His hand came away clean.

"Here, you take a look," he said.

While I peered into Keeyla's mouth, Terry studied the lamb lying in the grass. He laid his hand on her still flank.

"She's not been dead long," he said. He walked slowly around the site of the attack, kneeling on the ground in different spots, looking for clues.

"I don't see anything in Keeyla's mouth," I said to Terry.

"That doesn't mean she didn't do it," he said. "This is either a dog or a coyote kill, and I don't see any signs of coyotes. Besides, if it had been a coyote, it would have carried the lamb away. Not just ripped it open."

He was right. Coyotes weren't wasteful.

"But what if Keeyla chased the coyote away right after it killed the lamb?" I said. "It wouldn't have had time to carry the lamb away if Keeyla saw it and chased it away."

"Well, you've got a point there," he conceded. "But I don't think we can let this go. We just can't trust her."

Terry took Keeyla by the collar, and I bent over the dead lamb. Just minutes earlier it had been part of that silly gang of moppets bounding across the pasture. What a terrible shame and waste of life. Maybe Leroy had been right. Maybe Keeyla should have been put down as soon as she started chasing the goats. But I just couldn't believe she had done it.

Terry looked again at Keeyla's teeth, paws, and mouth. There was nothing: no evidence to either condemn or acquit her. She was either a killer or a hero. We would never know the truth.

Once again, Terry and I reached a compromise. Keeyla's life would be spared, but unless she was on a short, stout leash, Keeyla would never leave the kennel again.

❋

When Bart, Petey, and Karsey were set free in the morning, Keeyla stayed alone in the kennel. Each day, her excitement and elation mounted when she saw me coming across the yard. She jumped high in the air, yelping and barking, anticipation and delight written all over her face. Smiling, wiggling, wagging, she leapt to lick my face through the chain link fence as I worked the latch. Then, after the other dogs ran out, a crushed, confused look came over her when I closed the gate in her face. Every morning it was the same. She never lost hope that she would be set free, and her disappointment was just as intense on the second day, and the tenth day, and the hundredth day. That was Keeyla's trouble. She never learned.

Marketing

I sat down at the kitchen table with a classified ad form from a sheep breeders' magazine situated squarely in front of me. The marketing of our lambs had been put on the back burner for far too long. I knew I needed to start actively selling our lambs and wool if I hoped to have any chance of showing a profit by the end of the year. The routine animal chores and my growing consulting business were keeping me busy every day, and it was becoming harder and harder to carve out any time to address the items on my shepherdess to-do list.

I paged through our official flock record book, which in reality was of one of Beth's or Jon's old algebra notebooks. Following the twenty or so dog-eared, penciled pages of algebraic formulas, equations, and aborted homework assignments, we kept a record of all births, deaths, sales, and other details for each ewe and her offspring.

The records included as much as we knew about the genetics and reproductive history of each animal. There were also notes on the physical traits and wool characteristics of each ewe. Wool color; fleece characteristics such as crimp, length, texture of the wool; and other significant facts were recorded. Ewes that consistently produced twins were favored over those who bore singletons.

In the preceding weeks I had traced the genetics of a couple of nice young Shetland ram lambs born to our flock that spring, and at last I was ready to write the for-sale ad. I had spent some time tracing the ancestry of Rosie, Ada, and Lloyd. Both Rosie and Lloyd came from respected, if not champion, bloodlines. They were registered, and we could trace their ancestry back for generations. Ada was Rosie's half-sister, but her background was not nearly as impressive as her bad-tempered sister's.

This was our fourth year of lambing. Over the course of those four years our purebred Shetland ewes Rosie and Ada had produced eleven live lambs. We were able to sell some of the ewe lambs to other breeders for modest prices, and the other female lambs we kept to build our own flock. The Shetland ram lambs were gelded and kept for wool production. We had never before actively marketed or advertised our Shetland lambs.

But now, we needed to start generating some serious income from the sheep. Given Buck's appearance, both Terry and I knew he had the potential to bring in some money if he were sold to the right buyer. A ram's overall conformation is made up of structure, balance, soundness, and the presence of desirable breed traits. Young Buck had the straight legs, deep body, well sprung rib cage, and bright eyes of a champion.

Beyond conforming to the basic breed standards, Buck just had a special aura about him. He had a particular grace and charisma that is rare in lambs of his age. His behavior was appropriate and predictable, and both of those traits are desirable in a breeding ram. From very early on, it was apparent Buck was destined for greatness. Rosie doted on Buck, and Rambling Rose loved him, wholeheartedly and without jealousy.

As the weeks passed, I began to pin my hopes on selling Buck for a good price. He was our only moorit Shetland ram lamb born that year. The gene that exhibits the moorit color is recessive, and at that time Buck's rich, vibrant red brown hue was uncommon in North American Shetlands.

Finishing the narrative portion of the ad, I slid a few pictures of Buck into the envelope, and then I walked out to the mailbox with the completed form. The ad would appear in the September issue of the magazine. By that time Buck would be old enough for prospective buyers to feel assured he would survive into adulthood and would likely fulfill his youthful promise. I could hardly wait to see what type of response the ad would bring. The sale of Buck could be just the breakthrough we needed.

Emma the rabbit, armed and dangerous

One day in early July, most of the animals were grazing peacefully in the far pasture. Tony and his sidekick Whiplash were on their own apart from the rest of the flock, resting under one of the shade trees just outside the door of the sheep shed. Tony nuzzled Whiplash and hummed contentedly.

Even though Whiplash was no longer a newborn, Tony still followed her everywhere, never letting her out of his sight. Whiplash seemed to return Tony's affections, too, almost as if he were her surrogate parent. They made a strange-looking pair, since the tiny Whiplash barely reached Tony's knee when they were both standing.

I was filling the sheep's water tank when the dogs began barking wildly, signaling the approach of a vehicle. A car appeared over the top of the hill and careened up the driveway. Gravel flew as the car screeched to a halt in front of the house.

Luan had arrived. The driver's door swung open and Tux

exploded out, nearly shredding Luan's clothing as he scrambled over her in his haste. He hit the ground running, galloping in circles, sniffing the lawn and looking eagerly about for something to chase.

Luan jumped out of the car and collared Tux in a steel grip. She dragged him—his legs braced and his talonlike toenails scrabbling to grab hold of the lawn—across the yard and shoved him into the dog kennel, where he proceeded to fling himself against the chain link fence, barking madly.

Luan, wobbling slightly on high heels, walked over to join me beside the sheep shed as I finished filling the water tank. She was dressed for an evening out.

She gestured toward Tony and Whiplash, still lying together in the shade. "You're the only people I know whose livestock have their own pets," Luan said.

"What's the occasion? You're pretty dressed up," I said.

"Can you keep Tux tonight?" Luan asked. "I've got someone coming over, and I don't want Tux jumping and slavering all over him on the first date."

I looked at her skeptically. "I thought you'd given up on men entirely."

"That was before I met Brad."

"Oh?"

"He's different than the others," she said. "He plays in a band."

"And that's a good thing?" I asked.

"They only play the oldies," she said. "It's not like he's Ozzy Osbourne."

"The last time we discussed this, you claimed you'd run naked and screaming into the street before you'd get involved with another man," I reminded her.

"Well," Luan said smugly, "It's okay then, because I actually did run screaming into the street last night. I wasn't completely naked, though. I was wearing my flannel nightgown."

She proceeded to tell me the rest of the story. "Tux woke me up last night at about midnight. I had to let him out to do his little job, you know. I don't even bother to put him on the leash when he goes out at night, because he's usually in such a hurry to get back into my warm bed that he just takes care of business and rushes right back inside.

"But last night while he was outside, he caught sight of a cat at the far end of the block. He was off and running. I was only wearing my nightgown, but I ran down the street after him, yelling, 'Tux! Tux! Get back here!' I don't think anyone saw me. Well, except for that busload of seniors coming back from the casino."

She finished by saying, "So, anyway, I did fulfill the part about running into the street screaming, so now I'm free to date again."

"Well, just be careful," I cautioned. "By the way, how did you catch Tux last night?" I knew he had escaped from Luan before, and he had left a wake of disaster behind him before returning home in the wee hours.

"Well, thank goodness, he came back about ten minutes later. He was freezing and wanting to get back under the electric blanket. I'm still sleeping on the couch, by the way. It was nothing like that other night when he was gone until dawn and had gotten into every trash can on the block. Some of the neighbors still aren't speaking to me."

I agreed to keep Tux for the evening and wished Luan well with her date. "Just don't forget to come back for that lunatic," I said, watching said lunatic violently hurl himself against the chain link fence.

-❋-

Meanwhile, I had work to do with my rabbits. Yes, we were in the rabbit business as well. Once while attending a work-related conference, I had met a woman who spun the wool of her angora rabbits. It sounded like a fascinating idea, and I arranged a visit to her farm. It was love at first sight when I saw her calm and beautiful French angora rabbits. I bought three breeding rabbits from my new friend, and I knew my family would be thrilled.

No one at home was as excited about the rabbits as I was. Terry and Chris thought the rabbits looked interesting, but not rousing enough to warrant much effort in the areas of feeding, watering, or grooming. So the rabbits became my project entirely.

The wool of an angora rabbit can be harvested about three times each year, either plucked by hand or cut off with a scissors or an electric shear. Either way, it doesn't harm the animal. I have even heard of a woman who spins angora wool directly off the rabbit as it is seated in her lap.

To get the best wool for spinning, one should pluck the rabbit when its wool is prime, just before it begins to shed. Because I always seem to have too many rabbits and too little time, I don't use that method. I harvest wool with a scissors, which allows me to do the harvesting on my time schedule rather than the rabbit's. Then I spin the wool into fluffy, lightweight skeins of yarn. Over the winter, I knit the angora yarn into warm, fuzzy mittens, scarves, and hats. The angora rabbits produce wool in a wide variety of colors: white, fawn, cinnamon, chestnut, black, and various shades of gray and brown.

The first three rabbits I bought settled in nicely and began to reproduce. Before long, though, I realized I needed some new blood. I learned that I could increase the quantity of wool being produced by introducing some new genetic material into my herd.

I met a mother and daughter team who raised angora rabbits. The mother spun and knitted the rabbits' wool as I did, and her daughter showed the animals at competitions all over the United States. These rabbits were national champions, and they were of a much higher caliber than those I had previously bought. I wanted to access those superior bloodlines, but I had to stay within my budget. So I bought a few rabbits with good genetics but who themselves were not of show quality. That was fine with me, since my only concern at that time was wool production.

My new rabbits produced lovely wool in copious amounts, but they all had disabilities or flaws that would disqualify them from competition. Vincent (named after Vincent van Gogh) had only one ear. Vincent's mother had bitten off his other ear during an overly zealous grooming session in his youth. Then there was Thelma, who would have made the perfect pirate if only she had a patch to wear over her empty eye socket.

These interesting characters served as my primary breeding stock for several years. But as Chris got older and began showing rabbits at the county fair, I was forced to invest in some animals that were in possession of all of their body parts.

Each of my rabbits had a unique personality. Some were timid and cowered at the back of the cage when humans approached, while others were outgoing, leaping into one's arms when the cage door was opened. Some were passive and others were aggressive, and one in particular had a well-developed sense of humor. Emma, a cinnamon-colored doe, always provided a few laughs when it was her turn on the grooming table.

To harvest wool, I first set the rabbit on a tall grooming table about two feet square. The small table top allowed a minimum of space for movement, encouraging the rabbit to sit still for grooming. I piled a brush, toenail clippers, and a pair of scissors at the edge of the table.

Most of the rabbits ignored these implements while their

beauty regimen was under way. Each rabbit reacted differently to being groomed. Some enjoyed the luxury of having their hair brushed and toenails clipped, while others gritted their teeth and endured it with grunting and stamping of feet. But only Emma used her vantage point on the table to launch attacks on her enemies.

When I groomed rabbits in the summer, I placed the table under a shady tree in the yard. Two or three of the dogs usually wandered over and lay down at my feet while I worked. Soon the dogs were fast asleep, but the rabbit on the grooming table remained wary. The rabbits recognized the dogs from their occasional visits to the rabbit shed, when the dogs ran up and down the aisles, barking at the terrified rabbits in their cages. The rabbits were not fond of the dogs.

Each time I groomed Emma, she peered over the edge of the table. If she spotted a dog lying near the table, she reached out to grab the brush or scissors with her teeth, then she leaned over the edge of the table and dropped her missile onto the unsuspecting victim.

The dogs reacted as if Emma had dropped a live grenade. They yelped and scurried away, tails between legs. From the safety of the shrubbery, the dogs cowered and peered owlishly out, trying to guess what possibly could have happened. But soon they had forgotten the incident, and they wandered back over and fell asleep at my feet again. Emma was waiting. She dropped her bomb, and the dogs repeated their terrified performance.

⚜

But that day, I should have known better than to groom rabbits when Tux was visiting—even though he was napping when I started. He had worn himself out and fallen asleep after Luan left. I wasn't surprised, since he had spent hours barking and throwing himself against the chain link panels of the dog kennel. But at last all was quiet, and it seemed like a good time to harvest the wool of a few rabbits whose coats were overgrown and nearly past their prime.

I set up the table in a shady spot before bringing Emma out. Emma was one of the rabbits who really enjoyed being groomed. She stretched out to her full length and relaxed on the table. I brushed and untangled all of the long wool covering her body. As I reached for the scissors to begin clipping, a commotion arose from the vicinity of the dog kennel. The two dogs sleeping at my feet awoke with a start. A dark figure came streaking across the lawn, heading directly for the table and the rabbit seated upon it.

It was Tux. Chris was right on his heels. As Tux reached the table, leaping and lunging at Emma, Chris made a valiant attempt to wrestle him to the ground. "I saw Tux in the kennel, and I thought I'd let him out for a run. I didn't know you were grooming rabbits," Chris apologized over the din of Tux's barking. Tux twisted free of Chris's grasp.

By nature, rabbits are timid. Their usual reaction to the threat of a predator is to run and hide. Any ordinary rabbit would have been terrified by Tux, but Emma appeared almost calm. She stood alert, ears erect, with her neck extended and nose twitching. She stared intently at Tux as he leapt in the air, his sharp teeth snapping in her face at the apex of each jump. I tried to gather her in my arms to protect her, but she evaded me. Emma had no desire to be rescued.

The other dogs were no challenge for Emma: she could frighten them again and again with her same old tricks. But she knew she may have met her match in Tux. Quickly and deliberately, Emma used her teeth to grasp the handle of the eight-inch scissors. She leaned over the edge of the table, scissors clenched in her teeth. Just at that moment, Tux made another lunge for the rabbit's head, and the sharp point of the scissors made contact with Tux's long nose. It was a direct hit.

Emma wore a smug look of satisfaction on her face as I carried her to safety in the rabbit shed.

Meanwhile, Tux ran crazily in circles around the yard, yelping in pain. When Chris and I finally caught him, we checked to see if he was injured. He had a spot of blood at the end of his nose and was feeling very sorry for himself.

Chris patted the head of the old terrier and said, "Tux, you're probably the only dog on the planet who's been attacked by an armed rabbit."

Whiplash goes to town

Shortly after Tux's humiliation at the hands of Emma, Terry returned home from work. As we started on the evening sheep chores, I told Terry about Tux's run-in with Emma. Although the dog was now safely confined to the kennel, the sheep were still agitated over Tux's noisy rampage. They were milling around the yard, upset and uneasy.

As he made his usual head count of the sheep, Terry noticed Whiplash was walking with a pronounced limp. Tony hovered nearby, trying to keep the other sheep from jostling her. Terry examined Whiplash's small legs and hooves, seeing no outward signs of damage.

Thinking Whiplash had likely been stepped on by one of the sheep in their upset over Tux, we assumed she had a bruised hoof and decided to wait a day or two to see if her limp would improve. But by the next morning, Whiplash's limp was much worse. She was a pitiful sight, limping around the sheep yard, unable to join in the games of the lawless lamb gang.

I called the vet clinic to see if the vet would be out in our area that day. His receptionist told me he was doing a small-animal clinic, and he would not be making farm visits until the following day. I thought about it for a moment, then asked the receptionist if I could bring Whiplash to the clinic, since she was small enough to transport in the car.

She said, "Well, we normally see only dogs, cats, and small household pets here at the clinic." But she agreed to set up an appointment for Whiplash that afternoon.

Terry had the truck at work that day, so the only mode of transportation available was the car, with its light tan leather upholstery. After a few minor skirmishes, I had Whiplash enclosed in a cardboard box. I fastened the lid securely and set the box on the back seat of the car. By the time we reached the end of the driveway, Whiplash had freed herself. She stood on the back seat, doing a slippery dance on the cream-colored upholstery. Despite her limp, she was able to cover the entire seat and the rear window with muddy hoofprints. Again and again, Whiplash struggled to climb into the driver's seat with me, and I pushed her back. Her high-pitched cries were almost deafening in the small car.

When we arrived at the vet clinic, I tucked Whiplash under my arm and walked in the front door. The waiting room was packed with people and their pets. Most of the patients were dogs. There were also a few cats, but Whiplash was definitely the only sheep in the room.

I took a seat and tried to become invisible. It was not easy to do with Whiplash's *baa*ing and thrashing and kicking. Before long, she had wriggled out of my arms. On her gimpy leg she managed to make her way down the row of pets and people seated in chairs against the wall. Whiplash paused in front of each one and examined every animal as if she were responsible for making a diagnosis. The elderly woman seated beside me asked, "What kind of dog is that? I've never seen one like it."

We were called into the vet's office, and he easily diag-
nosed Whiplash's problem. An infection had entered her system through her navel when she was newly born, and it was
now affecting her joints. The vet gave Whiplash a dose of antibiotics and a steroid to ease her joint pain. Now docile, Whiplash took the doses without complaint. The vet gave me a few
syringes of the steroid to administer at home, and he said she
would be as good as new in no time. He was right.

"It's no use trying to get you back into that box, is it?" I
asked Whiplash as we headed for the car. I set her on the back
seat. With the drugs already taking effect, Whiplash had suddenly regained her high spirits, jumping about in the back of
the car as I drove away. She wedged herself into the space between the front bucket seats and nudged my arm, begging for
attention. After sucking noisily on my elbow for a minute, she
returned to the back seat and then climbed onto the shelf of
the rear window.

Whiplash had never before left the farm, and she was
captivated by all the new sights. When we stopped at a red
light, she tapped her hoof on the rear window, almost as if she
were waving to the people in the car behind us. I could see
the people in the vehicles around us laughing and pointing.
Finally the light changed to green, and we sped home.

When I lifted her out of the car, Whiplash was like a new
lamb. Almost all signs of her stiffness and joint pain were
gone. Tony was elated at Whiplash's return, and he met her at
the gate, humming happily and nuzzling her small body.

Identity crisis

Even at midsummer of her first year, Lamb Chop was still small enough to squeeze in and out of the pasture gate at will. She preferred the company of humans, and she sought us out wherever we happened to be. Time after time, we returned her to the sheep shed or the pasture and firmly placed her inside, only to discover her standing outside the kitchen door minutes later. When the kitchen door opened, she bounded up the steps and forced her way into the house.

People have said that when I pulled Lamb Chop out of the haystack shortly after her birth, the newborn "imprinted" on me—in other words, she bonded with me almost as a surrogate mother. Though I don't believe Lamb Chop's was a textbook example of imprinting, she certainly did form a strong bond with our family. She simply didn't believe she was a sheep. She used every trick in the book to escape from the shed or pasture and return to the human world where she felt she belonged.

Some summer days when Chris went to his friends' homes to play, Lamb Chop moped around the yard until he returned.

On the days when Chris wasn't around to keep Lamb Chop company, I tried to accustom her to staying in the pasture with the rest of the sheep. As she grew, it took all my might to push Lamb Chop back through the open gate. Once I had her bulk on the other side of the gate, I slammed it shut, fastened it, then turned and started back toward the house. Before I was halfway there, Lamb Chop had squeezed through the gate, raced past me, and disappeared around the corner of the house. When I reached the kitchen door, Lamb Chop stood waiting for me to let her in, as if she were a neighbor lady stopping by for a cup of coffee.

When no people were outside, Lamb Chop hung out with the dogs. She picked up many of their bad habits: the dogs had plenty of them, and they were more than willing to share. Before long, Lamb Chop was chasing cars right along with the rest of the pack. Lamb Chop was not as fleet-of-foot as the dogs, and she could never keep up with a car all the way to the end of the driveway. Her inability to bark was also a handicap in the car-chasing community. But Lamb Chop did her best, and she became quite adept at the dogs' favorite sport.

When Lamb Chop wasn't chasing cars, she was trying to squeeze herself into them. Few door-to-door salesmen were brave enough to open their car doors in the face of Karsey. But those who did found themselves battling a half-grown lamb that was struggling to get into their cars just as frantically as they were scrambling to get out.

Lamb Chop saw any open door as an invitation. She entered houses, cars, trucks, and travel trailers, shocking unwary occupants. And once inside, it was not easy to get her out.

My biggest concern for Lamb Chop was how she would cope when she grew too big to squeeze through the pasture gate. Terry's words often came back to haunt me: "You won't be doing her a favor by making a bottle lamb out of her."

Lamb Chop would be devastated when she could no longer spend her days with people and dogs. When winter came, she would need to live in the shed with the other sheep for her own warmth and safety. The following spring she would be expected to produce a lamb and care for it responsibly, just like all the other ewes. Lamb Chop would soon be forced to rejoin the flock permanently, whether she liked it or not.

Elmo the bird

One of the highlights of that summer was my mother's seventy-fifth birthday party. My mother had been a strict but loving parent when I was young, and she felt responsible for seeing that her children were raised right. At least she sincerely gave it her best shot. Our home was filled with fun and laughter, but Ma made sure we behaved ourselves.

So I was surprised at her indulgence with her grandchildren. But in a way it made sense—the grandchildren weren't a responsibility for her, they were sheer pleasure. She didn't have to worry about whether they ate vegetables, went to bed on time, or minded their manners. Her role was simply to love and enjoy them, and she did that to the fullest.

Grandma bought her grandchildren all the toys and games that Terry and I refused to buy, especially those we considered too violent or too expensive. She bought these forbidden items and kept them at her house for whenever Beth, Jon, and Chris visited. She let them eat whatever they wanted and watch whatever they wanted on television. When they visited, she told them outrageous stories of things she had done in her youth.

Grandpa gave them a male version of the same indulgence. He allowed Beth and Jon to drive his old pickup truck as soon as they were tall enough to see over the steering wheel. Jon mastered this feat when he was in kindergarten.

As Grandma's birthday party approached, Beth and I put together displays of pictures representing the seventy-five years of her life. While we were sorting through a pile of old pictures, Beth said, "Look, Mom! Remember this?" She held up a dog eared photo of a small blue green bird in a cage. Beside the cage stood a grim-looking Grandma. Indeed, the parakeet proved to be the test of her grandmotherly devotion, stretching even that tolerant woman to her limits.

❈

When Jon was twelve years old, he acquired a parakeet named Elmo. Depleting his meager savings, Jon bought Elmo an assortment of shiny toys, treats, and a new cage that sat on a small table in our kitchen. After he settled in to this new environment, Elmo seemed happy enough to me, and I assumed that he was living an ideal, carefree bird's life.

But looking back, I'm sure Elmo suffered from stress, and he must have experienced some serious anxiety attacks. Two-year-old Chris was fascinated by the bird. Chris watched others in the family whistling to Elmo, trying to teach him to imitate the sound. Not to be outdone, Chris stood beside the cage, doing his wet, sloppy version of a whistle, aimed directly at Elmo. The unhappy recipient of Christopher's affection sat dejectedly on his perch, his feathers dripping with well-intentioned saliva.

Not only was Elmo forced to tolerate the attentions of a small child, he also had to cope with several feline admirers.

The house cats took an intense interest in Elmo. They were not just your typical bird watchers, either. They were bent on eating Elmo for lunch. The cats spent hours sitting or lying beside his cage, licking their chops. Though I knew they couldn't fit their paws between the bars of the cage, poor Elmo didn't share that comforting knowledge. No matter how many times they tried and failed, the cats never gave up trying to murder Elmo. Elmo responded by scolding the cats as he hopped angrily from perch to perch.

When Elmo was about a year old, we decided to take a two-week family vacation. We had no livestock at that time, and Terry's parents would take care of our dogs and cats. But we couldn't leave Elmo in the house alone with the cats. What to do?

The logical solution was to take Elmo to Grandma's for safekeeping. My mother had moved into an apartment in town following the death of my dad. There was just one catch: though she had lived on a farm for most of her life, Grandma never liked animals. She never owned a house pet, and she particularly disliked birds. For many years, my mother raised chickens and sold eggs to supplement the farm income. She was not fond of the hens. Being pecked by chickens was an occupational hazard back in the days when eggs were gathered by hand. Each day, my mother reached under the warm feathery bodies of over a hundred chickens and tried to remove their eggs without arousing the wrath of the squawking hens. After decades of living and working on the farm, Grandma claimed she would die a happy woman if she never had to lay eyes on anything resembling a chicken again.

So she wasn't enthusiastic about taking on the care of Elmo, even temporarily. It was with great trepidation that we asked, and it was with grudging acceptance that Grandma agreed to keep Elmo for us. We dropped off Elmo and all of his paraphernalia the night before we left on vacation. Grandma looked overwhelmed by the boxes and bags of food, treats, and toys that the well-supplied bird required.

While we were gone, Grandma stationed Elmo's cage on a chair beside the television. Elmo didn't respond well to this disruption of his routine. Feathers flew everywhere as he dashed from perch to perch in the cage, screeching. Grandma winced at the noise, and she cranked up the TV's volume to drown out Elmo's piercing cries. Elmo retaliated by shrieking even louder and beating his wings against the bars of the cage.

When we returned from vacation, we were curious to hear how things had gone for Grandma and Elmo. I called her shortly after we got home. When she answered the phone I could hear Elmo chattering raucously in the background. "When can you come and pick up this damn bird?" my mother asked. "I don't know how much longer I can stand the commotion."

"I've got a lot of things to catch up on here, but I'll come as soon as I can," I told her. We didn't make the trip into town for nearly a week.

Frankly, I was in no hurry to get Elmo back. I was relieved at not having to sweep the birdseed and feathers off the kitchen floor every morning. I didn't miss Elmo's screams while I tried to talk on the phone. In fact, I tend to share my mother's attitude toward birds, probably because of all of those angry rooster attacks and egg-picking episodes in my own youth.

The following week Jon and I stopped at Grandma's to pick up Elmo. Jon was looking forward to having the bird back at home, and my conscience told me we shouldn't leave him there any longer. We gathered up the boxes of food, treats, and toys and prepared to load them into our car. Jon carried Elmo's cage. Elmo dangled upside down from a perch, squawking loudly. But just as we were heading out the door, a light rain began to fall. We waited a few minutes to see if it would let up, but the rain increased to a steady downpour. Elmo would be drenched if we carried him to the car. I turned to my mother and asked, "Would you mind keeping Elmo for another few days? Just until we can get back to town?"

Though she said nothing in response, she nodded her head. Jon reluctantly set Elmo's cage back down beside the TV, and we dashed through the rain to the car and drove home, birdless.

Similar scenes played out over the next few weeks whenever we stopped at Grandma's. It seemed there was always some good reason why we couldn't bring Elmo home. One week I painted the kitchen, and I was convinced the paint smell would be bad for Elmo. On each following occasion I came up with some flimsy excuse, saying it was either too hot, too cold, too humid, or too late in the evening for Elmo to safely navigate the distance from Grandma's apartment to our car in the parking lot.

Days turned into weeks, weeks into months, and still we hadn't brought Elmo home. With glum determination, Grandma continued to care for her unwanted house guest. She cleaned up Elmo's daily messes of feathers and birdseed and tended to his needs, but she showed no affection toward him—unless one could consider the phrase "Shut up, you damn bird!" an endearment.

The same could not be said for Elmo. It was plain to see that Elmo loved Grandma, and he flourished under her care. The absence of cats and small children acted like a tonic for Elmo, and he became a whole new bird. Gone was the tortured, angry scold. In its place was a bright, cheerful creature who sang happily and chattered constantly to his new companion. He was utterly devoted to Grandma. As we observed this, our offers to take Elmo home became less frequent, and gradually they dwindled away completely. Grandma's birdsitting job continued for two years.

Then one day Grandma was admitted to the hospital for surgery. She would need to stay there for more than a week. My brother Joe lived only a few blocks away from her apartment, and he volunteered to look in on Elmo.

When Joe first checked on the bird, there was none of the squawking or shrieking that usually greeted a visitor's arrival. Moreover, Joe told me, Elmo hadn't been eating. I wasn't very concerned, thinking Elmo was probably just having an off day. But when this behavior stretched into midweek, we all became worried.

The whole family stopped in at Grandma's apartment to see if we could tempt Elmo to eat. Jon offered him his favorite foods, but he showed no interest. Elmo stood silently on his perch, staring straight ahead. The only discernible movement was an occasional blink of his beady eye.

In the following days, Joe dropped in daily to pick up Grandma's mail and to check on Elmo. When he heard the apartment door opening, Elmo turned his head eagerly to see who was there. When he saw it wasn't Grandma, he resumed his stony silence and blank stare.

The mute blue green figure was unrecognizable as the Elmo of yore. Elmo—during his years under Grandma's regime—loved life, and he lived it with the utmost exuberance and flair. We could think of no way to communicate to Elmo that Grandma would soon be home. Our only hope was that he could hold on until she returned from the hospital.

The day before Grandma was scheduled to be released, Joe called with an update. The message he left on our answering machine was short and to the point. "Elmo has died of a broken heart."

※

Though I was sad to hear about Elmo, I had to admit his demise had come at an opportune time. After her surgery

Grandma probably wasn't feeling up to the never-ending round of cleaning, feeding, and entertaining that Elmo demanded. Certainly she would see his death as a reprieve and a release from an unwanted duty.

Joe planned to drive Grandma home from the hospital and see that she was comfortable and settled back at her apartment. When I got home from work that evening, I called Joe to see how the day had gone. Being a bachelor, he wasn't always attuned to the finer nuances of housekeeping. I hoped he had removed the dead body of Elmo before Grandma returned home.

"You did bury Elmo before Ma got home, didn't you?" I asked when Joe answered the phone that evening.

"Umm—not exactly. I guess you could say Elmo was buried at sea," he said. I thought it best not to pursue that line of questioning any further. Instead I asked how Grandma's homecoming had gone.

"Well, it was strange. As soon as she got into the car at the hospital, she asked about Elmo," said Joe. "She said, 'I suppose that damn bird has made a mess all over my floor, the way he scatters seeds everywhere.' So I told her what happened. I thought she'd be relieved to be through cleaning up after that old bird." Joe went on to describe Grandma's response to the news: there was no visible reaction, but she sat in silence for the remainder of the drive home. When she entered her apartment, Grandma glanced briefly at the empty cage, still sitting beside the television. The door hung open, and a few blue green feathers were strewn across the carpet. Joe said, "I'll take that cage out to the car now and get it out of your way."

As Joe left the apartment, Grandma sat gazing at the flickering television screen in a manner which he described as being oddly reminiscent of Elmo's vacant stare during his last days.

Physically, Grandma recovered from her surgery. But it was obvious to all who knew her that the feisty old woman had lost some of her spark. The world had lost a bit of its color and life a bit of its appeal for the woman who hated birds.

＊

I still felt occasional twinges of guilt at having foisted Elmo upon Grandma all those years ago. Maybe that's part of the reason I volunteered to host a family reunion in honor of her seventy-fifth birthday.

The day of the party dawned bright and sunny. Grandma's sisters, nieces, and nephews from as far away as California gathered at our place to celebrate. Since it was such a beautiful day, we decided to eat outside. Terry arranged chairs and tables on the lawn at the back of the house, and Beth and I carried plates of food and pitchers of lemonade from the kitchen. As a precaution, the cats had been dispatched on a short vacation to the Hamptons. The Nerf gun had been packed away for the day, and I could think of no other way to keep Tinkles under control.

Beth and I finished serving the guests, and I looked around with satisfaction. Everything was going well. The weather was perfect, Grandma was enjoying the day, and for once it seemed that we were going to be able to have a peaceful meal without being interrupted by the animals.

My euphoria was shattered by a crash as one of the guests screamed and dropped her plate of food onto the sidewalk. Lamb Chop appeared out of nowhere, rounding the corner of the house at full speed. The youngest children shrieked and scattered, and the adults rose to their feet in alarm as the half-grown sheep sprinted through their midst.

Dodging picnic tables and old women in lawn chairs, Lamb Chop clattered up the back steps and came to a halt on the deck outside the kitchen door. Lamb Chop had crashed the party.

Terry and I caught her by her thick fleece before she could do any more damage. As we forced her down the steps, Terry said to me, "You know that nothing short of a miracle is going to keep her away now that she knows there's a party going on, don't you?"

I agreed there was no point in trying to return Lamb Chop to the pasture or shed. Between the two of us, we were able to drag her to the bottom of the steps. I held the sheep still while Terry turned to the guests and apologized.

He explained that Lamb Chop was experiencing an identity crisis. "She believes she's human," he said. He told the guests to ignore her. "With any luck, she'll wander back to the shed. You won't even know she's here."

The relatives sat down again and resumed eating. Terry's speech did little to reassure them. Throughout the rest of the afternoon, the guests continued to scan the horizon in fear of what might appear next to stampede through their reunion.

Contrary to Terry's prediction, Lamb Chop did not wander back to the shed. She mingled. She grazed on watermelon and cake. She posed for pictures. She supervised game after game of croquet and badminton. She spent an hour wedged into a double-wide lawn chair between two girls from Grand Forks, North Dakota. Lamb Chop enjoyed the reunion immensely, and she appears in all the family photos taken that day.

The nature of sheep

W hen Rambling Rose was first let out on pasture, most of the other sheep were rough and impatient with her, but her mother simply left her alone. Rosie didn't mistreat her blind lamb, but she didn't go out of her way to protect her, either. She mostly ignored Rose and lavished her attention on Buck.

Buck continued to shape up well. Terry and I watched him develop, knowing he showed real promise. He was robustly healthy and good-natured, and—like icing on the cake—Buck's moorit fleece was coming in exceptionally fine and soft.

By this time, too, it had become clear that Rambling Rose was far from normal. She couldn't walk a straight line, listing off to one side as she traveled across the sheep yard like a drunken sailor. She tended to gain momentum as she moved, and she went faster and faster until she collided with something solid. After the impact, Rose would shake herself off and start over again.

Rambling Rose had an odd look about her—even apart from her unsteady gait, her jauntily cocked head, and opaque sightless eyes. Her top lip was perpetually drawn up—almost as if she were squinting—and a tiny row of teeth was exposed.

The other sheep tolerated Rose, much as one might put up with an irritating relative who has come for an extended visit. They became used to her odd behavior, and soon they took little notice of her activities.

When I came home from town one day, I stopped the car to watch the sheep as they grazed in the pasture along the driveway. During the spring and summer months we are constantly counting the sheep to make sure no lambs have wandered off or been taken by coyotes. But it is mostly for pleasure that I watch the sheep. I wonder what they're thinking about as they stand or lie gazing silently ahead at nothing. This day was no different.

The sheep ceased their grazing and moved to lie down in the shade of the tall, leafy ash trees. All of the sheep had settled down for an afternoon rest. All, that is, except Rambling Rose. Since her mother had lain down, the bell around her neck was silent. And when the bell was silent, Rose became frantic. One bleat from Rosie would have reassured her daughter, but Rosie just continued to lie silently, chewing her cud and contemplating the universe.

Meanwhile, Rambling Rose was stumbling through the collection of resting bodies, crying out for her mother, tripping over four or five of them in her haste. She buried her head in one fleece after another as the ewes calmly stared off into the distance. I often wondered why the sheep didn't react more strongly to being accosted so rudely, but they seemed to have acquired an ability to tune out any unpleasant stimuli— which described Rambling Rose to a tee.

—✳—

Every evening at dusk, all of the sheep slowly worked their way toward the sheep shed for the night. They entered through a door that stood about two feet ajar: enough to ventilate the shed but keep out the wind and rain. Rosie, Buck, and the other sheep crowded effortlessly through the opening in a rush to be first to the hay feeder or the salt block. But every evening Rambling Rose was left outside alone after the other sheep had pushed their way through, and every evening she struggled to navigate the narrow opening.

Rosie made only one small concession for her blind daughter. When she entered the shed in the evening, she stood just inside the door and called to Rambling Rose. Like a rusty foghorn, the hoarse calls of the crabby ewe guided her lamb to shelter. Hearing her mother's voice and clanging bell, the lamb headed in the general direction of the shed door. But because of the tilt of her head, she consistently veered to the left, missing the narrow opening time and again. After each miss, Rambling Rose circled around again like an airplane coming in for a landing, Rosie's rasping *baaaaa* guiding her like a beacon. The lamb missed her target by a smaller margin on each pass until she finally made it through the narrow doorway and was safely inside for the night.

That summer Chris and I watched over Rambling Rose, making sure she was keeping up as the flock migrated between the three pastures. Many times each day we carried her to the water trough just outside the sheep shed. Rambling Rose could smell the cool water from quite a distance, and her pink nose twitched as she neared the trough. She drank long and deeply before turning back to the pasture and tottering off in response to the sound of her mother's bell.

A blind lamb has absolutely no commercial value. Rambling Rose didn't have a high-quality fleece, and she was so small that she would be worthless as a feeder lamb. As shepherds, we should have been investing our time and devoting our attention to the young sheep that would become next year's wool and lamb producers—not spending hours teaching a blind lamb how to find the shed door or the water trough. Just keeping Rambling Rose alive would be costly and time-consuming. It made no practical sense at all.

"Dad says it's sometimes kindest to put down lambs if they are suffering," Chris said as we watched the evening ritual: Rambling Rose was struggling to find her way through the narrow opening of the shed door.

"Do you think Rose is suffering?" I asked him. I was sincerely interested in his opinion, because I grappled with that same question every day.

"Well, she doesn't have much of a future," he said. "But, no. I really don't think she is suffering. When I hold her, or when she's lying beside Rosie, I think she is as happy as a sheep can be."

He was right. She may not have experienced the same quality of life as the other lambs, but Rose often seemed to find a rare contentment, especially when she was lying safely up against her mother's solid bulk in the evening. As long as the moments of contentment outweighed the times of frustration and fear, I felt we were justified in keeping her alive.

Rose's heart's desire was to lie still beside cantankerous old Rosie in the evening. When the sheep settled down in the shed for the night, the blind lamb could finally relax. Rosie parked herself in one spot, where she would remain unmoved until morning. Her daughter didn't have to stay constantly vigilant, listening for the sound of the bell, as she did during the daytime. She snuggled up tightly beside her mother, and Buck was tucked close on Rosie's other side. The blind lamb's small, worried face took on a peaceful aspect, and she slept soundly. There was no doubt about it. Rambling Rose was content in the evenings.

※

Judging by their behavior, sheep often seem devoid of any feelings of empathy, compassion, or even common decency. This lack is especially evident whenever food is involved. If you set a bale of hay before a flock of sheep on a cold winter morning, it's every ewe for herself.

There are no words in sheep vernacular for "Excuse me," "After you," or "Sorry, was that your foot I stepped on?" Instead it is a fierce competition for the prime spots at the feed bunk. Those who get there first are often subject to violent head butts in their wooly flanks by others hoping to usurp the best places at the feeder.

Some sheep have a gentler nature, but others, like Rosie, would take any opportunity to waylay the random human or animal that happened to be nearby when she was having a bad day.

Rambling Rose was the only sheep I have ever known who was truly good. Lamb Chop and Whiplash were sweet and tame, but—like most lambs—they both had a devilish streak. Not Rambling Rose. She was unfailingly gentle and kind. Unlike the other sheep, cats, dogs, and various animals on our farm, Rambling Rose had no ulterior motives, showed no aggression, and bore no grudges.

Terry and I disagree about the nature of sheep. I believe the sheep have thoughts, emotions, and feelings similar to humans', while Terry claims they are motivated solely by basic instincts such as hunger and fear. Though he is too tactful to say it, I know Terry is of the opinion that I spend far too much time analyzing the thoughts and motivations of sheep and not nearly enough time hauling hay or shoveling manure.

❊

Sheep are creatures of habit. They like to do the same things at the same time every day, rain or shine, winter or summer. And they like to do the same things in exactly the same way every time.

The deep trails that criss-cross the pasture are one example of the sheep's love of routine. When the sheep are in their grazing mode, they fan out into the pasture in a random pattern. But when it's time to move to the far pasture, or to return home for their ritualistic afternoon drink of water, or to go into the sheep shed for the night—precisely at dusk—they don't move randomly. They line up in an orderly fashion and proceed to the nearest well-worn path. Then they trudge in single file ever-so-slowly-and-deliberately, never setting foot off the narrow path until they reach their destination.

Our sheep are such creatures of habit that they lie in the place where they are used to finding shade, whether the shade is there or not. On hot summer days, they vie for the best spots under the few big shade trees in the pasture. By the time everyone has settled down for their afternoon rest on a sunny day, the shape of the flock is identical to the shape of the shade.

One cold but sunny winter day I noticed the sheep were lying under those same trees in the snowless pasture, where they still spent their afternoons. I wondered about the strange pattern they made, lying on the brown dry grass under the bare trees. Anyone with a bit of sense would have sought a sheltered place out of the wind to lie down.

But then I understood. The sheep had positioned themselves under the trees as if they were seeking shade, just as they did on hot summer days. Maybe the bright sun had triggered the reaction. For whatever reason, the sheep liked to stick to a routine.

The flock *always* ceased grazing precisely at dusk and walked single file down the path to the sheep shed for the night. The llama, alpaca, and sheep were instinctively aware of the presence of coyotes and other nocturnal dangers. Even on the hottest summer evenings, they crowded into the shed and lay down.

After the sheep migrated back to the shed at dusk, either Terry or I would close the heavy door and bolt it shut. Nothing could get in or out once the door was bolted. It made all of us feel secure.

Drought

ike almost all of the other farmers around us, we were feeding hay in early July that year. We'd had no rain in weeks, and the grass was brown and brittle underfoot by midsummer. In a typical year, our sheep can thrive on pasture grass alone well into September or even early October. It was hard to watch Terry pitching forkful after forkful of this valuable commodity into the sheep feeders just after the fourth of July.

Not only was the pasture dried up and unproductive, it looked like we would be seriously short of hay for the coming winter. In desperation, Terry and I cut and baled everything that might be considered remotely palatable by the livestock, including patches of weeds, thistles, and the slough grass from a dried-up water hole. All of this yielded a mere fifty-five bales. Terry was worried.

The situation was the same for cattle and sheep producers throughout our area. Farmers were selling as many animals as they could. There simply wasn't enough pasture for them, and there wouldn't be enough hay to get them through the coming winter.

Terry hauled a trailer load of crossbred lambs to the auction barn in Fergus Falls in late July. We didn't have enough pasture to feed them any longer.

An enclave of immigrants now lived in the Pelican Rapids area, and they were usually in the market for lamb meat. In recent years that had improved the price paid for our biggest crossbred lambs. But the price we got that July was pitiful. It barely paid for the gas to haul them to the sale. The livestock market was flooded with animals, and that drove the price down to rock bottom.

Our purebred Shetland lambs were valuable, but only if we could find the right buyers. The Icelandic crossbred lambs were usually sold as feeders—that is, for meat. For flocks yielding wool of hand-spinning quality, our area had no established market for selling either the wool or the lambs. To get better prices for our Shetland lambs, we would need to be far more visible in a larger marketplace. Breeders who got the top prices showed their sheep nationally and even internationally, and they were well known in the heritage sheep community. It takes a huge amount of time and travel to develop a presence in the nationwide market. Since our small flock had until recently been merely a hobby, we hadn't made much effort in marketing either our wool or our breeding stock.

But even without advertising, every year we'd managed to sell some of our purebred Shetland lambs as breeding stock. Those buyers just seemed to be able to find us. A few of the crossbred lambs were sold to weavers or spinners or as lawn ornaments to retired farmers who just wanted to keep a few animals on a small acreage. One of my main objectives was to sell fewer lambs as feeders and more for breeding or wool producers. But in my first year of professional shepherding, we were forced to sell dozens of lambs to the slaughter market.

Coyotes, Mack Dawg, and Camilla

In our area, coyotes are the most common and most serious predator of small livestock. Coyotes are rarely seen by humans, though the howls and yips of these predators can often be heard at dusk and throughout the night. It is said the word *coyote* is derived from an ancient Aztec term meaning singing dog, which is an accurate description of the eerie lament of these sheep-eating varmints.

When coyotes attack adult sheep, they typically bite the throat just behind the jaw. Death usually results from suffocation and shock. For smaller prey, like lambs, coyotes kill by biting the head, neck, or back, causing massive tissue damage. Young lambs are sometimes carried away whole by coyotes, disappearing without a trace. By the time the shepherd arrives on the scene, there is no carcass, no sign of struggle, no trail of blood. Often the only evidence of a coyote kill is the frantic bleat of a ewe searching for her missing lamb.

Though they are always a concern for shepherds, the coyotes were particularly troublesome that summer. An elderly

neighbor lost over half of his spring lambs to the wily predators: he claimed that the coyotes even came up into the farmyard in broad daylight searching for food. The recent drought
had intensified the problem. The mice and rabbits that made
up the coyotes' usual diet had left for greener pastures, and
the pickings were slim. Many animals, both domestic and
wild, went hungry that season.

All summer we worried that the coyotes would take the
bumbling and vulnerable Rambling Rose. She made an easy
mark. The sheep spent their nights in the safety of the shed,
but there was no guarantee that a coyote, desperate and hungry, wouldn't sneak down out of the hills and carry Rose away
during the daylight hours.

Every morning when I woke, I looked out the north-facing
window of our bedroom. If I could see the dark blob of Black
Betty staked out in our neighbor's meadow and the two
smaller blobs of her kids nearby, I took it as a good omen. The
goats had escaped the night's coyote raid and would live to
see another day.

Eventually, Terry agreed to my proposed solution to the
coyote problem. I was convinced we needed another guard
llama. We realized that Camilla the llama and Tony the alpaca were both worthless as sheep protectors—for two rea-
sons. First, we had acquired them as adult animals. Since
they hadn't grown up as part of the flock, they lacked any
protective instincts toward it. Second, if you have more than
one llama or alpaca, they will tend to form their own herd,
even amidst a sheep flock. Enjoying their cozy clique, they
couldn't care less if a predator carries away the entire flock.
We had seen evidence of this behavior with our own animals.
If a neighbor's dog got into the pasture and started chasing
sheep, Tony and Camilla hightailed it off to the shed, leaving
the flock behind in the dust without a second thought.

So a single, young animal was what we wanted in a flock

guardian. And our acquaintances George and Iris just happened to have a young male llama they were willing to sell. Socks was a sable brown yearling who was tame and friendly. He had been raised as a family pet. He was just over a year old, still young enough to be capable of bonding with the sheep flock.

"Are you sure you don't have some ulterior motive?" Terry asked. "I'm surprised at your sudden interest in getting another llama."

"I am dead serious about finding a solution to the coyote problem," I said. "We can't afford to lose any more lambs." But as usual, Terry had seen through to the heart of the matter. Socks would be a perfect mate for Camilla.

"Maybe there is another reason," I admitted. "Just think about it, Terry. We can make baby llamas and sell them. Certainly that'll improve our bottom line. It's a sure moneymaker."

He didn't look convinced, so I continued. "Besides, getting a guard llama is like buying insurance to protect our livestock investment. We're going to take the animal business more seriously now, remember?"

After some further arm-twisting, Terry agreed to the purchase, and we called George to close the deal. George said he would deliver Socks, the young guardian llama, the following day.

❊

Terry, Chris, and I were waiting in the yard when George arrived with the llama. Before Socks even got out of the livestock trailer, Chris announced the animal would no longer be called Socks. Rather, his new name would be Mack Dawg, after the snowboard filmmaker.

Our three children usually took the naming of the animals upon themselves. When they were younger, the names

they chose for kittens and puppies were cute and inoffen-
sive—names like Spot, Buttons, or Petey. As they got older,
their name selections grew edgier. When they reached their
teen years, the kids' choices expanded to include rap musi-
cians and extreme sports stars. And it wasn't unusual, at the
end of an ill-fated romance, for a particularly unappealing
sheep to wind up with the name of someone's ex-boyfriend
or -girlfriend.

Even while he was still in the trailer, Mack Dawg exuded
the powerful, musky odor of the intact male. The sheep in the
nearby pasture pricked up their ears and sniffed the wind,
craning their necks and looking in all directions to see what
was afoot. Camilla was positively riveted by the distinctive
scent of the male of her species.

Terry and I agreed we would first see to the mating, and
then Mack Dawg would be isolated with the sheep. If we kept
Mack separate from Tony and Camilla, we were sure he would
soon bond with the sheep and become their protector.

We unloaded Mack into a small pen near the barn and
then led Camilla over to join him. The dating game got under
way immediately. George, Terry, Chris, and I stood off at a distance, watching the ritual unfold.

Mack and Camilla's first encounter was celebrated with
much screaming and general hysteria. None of these were
screams of joy or elation, as far as I could tell. Both of the llamas were first-time breeders, and thus inexperienced. Ide-
ally one would use an experienced male for the first breeding
of a young female, and vice versa. Since we had only two llamas at our disposal, our options were limited.

After a short period of spitting, braying, and neck wres-
tling, the two llamas got down to business. Copulation takes
place while the female llama is kushing, or lying down. The
male then gets into position and begins what the experts
term his orgling call: a loud, buzzing gargle. Mack Dawg's

orgling call was piercingly shrill. This earsplitting drone echoed through the barnyard for nearly an hour, far longer than it took him to complete the actual deed.

The gestation period of a llama is eleven months and three weeks. It would be months before we would know whether the mating would bear fruit.

Chris was twelve years old when Mack and Camilla consummated their union. He watched enthralled as the noisy and elaborate mating ceremony played out, and I wondered—not for the first time—if we were inflicting untold damage upon his young and tender psyche. For better or worse, Chris has experienced firsthand many of nature's wonders: witnessing the miracle of birth, watching as newborn lambs take their first steps. Now he could add to that list his observation of the mating of the South American beast of burden. How better could we have prepared our child for life in the twenty-first century?

Terry and I assumed once the mating was completed we would move Camilla to a separate, distant pasture. We would then transfer Mack to the sheep pasture, where he would attach himself to the flock and assume his new position as guard llama. We had it all figured out.

Tux and Daisy

Compared to that of Camilla and Mack, the courtship of Luan and Brad was progressing with dignity and decorum. It came as no surprise to learn the only fly in the ointment was Tux.

Since Brad lived in Minneapolis and Luan lived in Glenwood, they saw each other only on weekends. Brad usually came to Luan's home on Friday night, and after dinner the two of them would rent and watch a movie. Luan got the movie started, then she sat beside Brad on the couch. But the fiercely jealous Tux insisted on sitting between them. If denied, he would whine, paw, pace, bark, and entirely ruin the evening for everyone.

So Brad began bringing Daisy, his aging and arthritic Chihuahua, when he visited Luan. He hoped Daisy's slow-as-molasses pace would act as a calming influence on Tux. The plan backfired. Tux's traits rubbed off on Daisy, instead of the other way around. So Brad and Luan ended up with two jealous and neurotic dogs firmly planted between them on the couch when they watched their evening movie.

The dogs ate the popcorn, guzzled Brad and Luan's drinks when no one was looking, and then eventually dozed off. By the close of the evening, the snores of the foul-smelling, slightly tipsy old dogs completely drowned out the sound of the movie. Not that it mattered. By that time the romantic ambiance had worn off.

Though Tux and Luan were getting along better, his hyperactivity still caused problems. Luan was constantly seeking solutions to Tux's troubles. She fed him yogurt three times a day for his sensitive digestive system and to help dispel the horrific gas attacks that sent everyone fleeing for cover. She peeled and fed him baby carrots, which she had heard might improve his foul breath. Luan bought a doggy toothbrush and chicken-flavored toothpaste, but during her first brushing of Tux's teeth she nearly lost a couple of fingers, so she gave up on his oral hygiene sessions.

Luan learned of a new herbal anti-anxiety medication for dogs, and she bought a huge bottle of the pills. A thirty-pound dog like Tux should have one tablet daily to take the edge off his excitement. Luan began treatment with three times the recommended dosage.

After a few failed attempts to get the pills down Tux's throat, Luan tried hiding them in his yogurt. Tux was too smart to be fooled by that old ruse, and he carefully lapped up the yogurt, leaving the pills untouched in the bottom of his bowl. But in his constant state of excitement, Tux could bear to leave no stone unturned, and he ended up running back to his dish and eating the pills anyway. Still, even the triple dose barely made a dent in Tux's enthusiasm.

The county fair

Chris and his friends worked on their building projects all summer. With Terry's help they built a dirt track for bike and motocross racing at the edge of a hayfield. The boys slaved for weeks in the hot summer sun, adding jumps to the oval track.

Visits to the hospital emergency room became embarrassingly frequent. Once while I sat with Chris in the emergency room, watching the doctor scrutinize the X-rays for broken bones, a thought occurred to me: Terry and I might be reported to the authorities for child abuse because of the number of bruises and abrasions covering the body of our child. But my fears were relieved when Chris lifted his head off the gurney and asked the doctor, "How soon can I get back on my skateboard?"

It was a relief when August rolled around and Chris had to get busy with his 4-H projects for the Douglas County Fair. He always waited until the last minute before he focused seriously on his projects, but once he started he worked like a man possessed.

The rabbits were groomed daily, and the other animals endured the required vaccinations. But the toughest job for Chris was halter breaking the lambs and teaching them to behave for the sheep show. He planned to show Lamb Chop in the crossbred ewe lamb class and Matilda, another spring lamb, in the purebred class.

Every evening, Terry and Chris captured the elusive Matilda. Then Matilda and the all-too-easy-to-catch Lamb Chop were strapped into show halters. Using the dogs' leashes, Chris walked the lambs up and down the driveway for an hour. These practice runs had to be undertaken in the evening when it was cool outside, because the lambs got themselves so worked up. Terry was concerned they would suffer heatstroke if it were done during the eighty- to ninety-degree temperatures of midday.

As soon as the halters were buckled on their heads, the two lambs planted their feet stubbornly and refused to budge. When Chris tugged on the leashes, the lambs rolled over onto their sides and played dead. They did everything possible to avoid cooperating with Chris as he tried to lead them down the road. It was hard to believe this was the same Lamb Chop who cheerfully trotted up and down the driveway all day long while chasing cars with the dogs.

After dragging, pleading, and often picking up and carrying one or both of the lambs, the boy reached the end of the driveway with his charges. Chris then turned around and headed for home. This move brought about an entire change of attitude for the lambs. On the return trip, the lambs strained at the leashes, leaped into the air, and nearly dragged Chris at a full gallop back to the yard.

One might assume that Chris participated in the county fair for the sake of gaining knowledge and experience, but in reality his motives were far less altruistic. The prize money earned from a few blue-ribbon lambs would go a long way toward buying new skateboard wheels or another load of lumber for bigger and better jumps.

In addition to showing sheep at the fair, Chris entered a variety of other projects, too. He is a talented photographer and artist, and he won many grand champion ribbons during his 4-H years. But it was Chris's shop projects that really stood out. They were unlike anything else at the fair.

The younger kids entered simple shop projects, like small table clocks made from kits. Every year dozens of these clocks lined the shelves of the exhibit hall. With some simple sawing, sanding, gluing, and varnishing and the insertion of a pre-made clock mechanism, these kids had an easy project, and the finished product was neat and attractive. The older kids built more complex things, such as oak cabinets, chairs, and desks.

In contrast, Chris's shop projects were ugly, visceral pieces, made of roughly hewn lumber and metal: massive skateboard ramps, rails, and platforms. Though you couldn't tell by looking at them, each one was a feat of design, engineering, and physics. They were mammoth in size, coarse and unfinished in appearance, but ingeniously designed to suit their purpose. In short, they stuck out like Jackson Pollock paintings hung among Norman Rockwell prints. Though they were not pleasing to the eye, they attracted plenty of attention from fairgoers. "What on earth is *that?*" they asked, looking puzzled and uneasy.

Each year, before entry day, the extension staff asked apprehensively, "What's Chris planning to bring to the fair this year?" To accommodate Chris's unorthodox projects, they needed to allow plenty of space, and they sometimes roped off an area for the safety of all concerned.

The 4-H shop judge, an experienced woodworker, examines each exhibit for workmanship and appearance. He interviews the exhibitor, testing the child's knowledge of construction techniques and use of materials and tools. Most of the exhibitors get blue ribbons—as long as they are relatively knowledgeable about the proper techniques and have a reasonably attractive product. A few red ribbons are given to those children with less knowledge or whose items have obvious flaws but who have at least made some visible effort. Very rarely, a judge will bestow a white ribbon. This happens when the exhibitor has clearly missed the mark by a wide margin.

On judging day, the big steel building at the fairgrounds was swarming with kids, parents, judges, and county extension staff. Chris and I were there in the crowd, carrying boxes of art, photography, and geology exhibits.

Chris joined the line of boys waiting for their shop projects to be judged. He was never very articulate with the judge during his interview, and I was afraid his ego would take a beating when, year after year, his shop projects scored low on the judges' rating scale. Terry and I debated whether we should even let him enter these peculiar creations. "Don't you want to make one of those nice little wooden clocks out of a kit?" I'd ask him.

That year Chris had built and entered a huge skateboard ramp. Constructed on a framework of two-by-four lumber and covered with sheets of plywood, it was braced underneath with salvaged pieces of welded scrap metal. The bead of the weld wasn't perfect, but Chris's intent was to make a strong weld, not a pretty one.

Terry hauled the ramp to the fairgrounds on his way to work that morning. When it was Chris's turn to talk with the judge, I waited at a discreet distance, where I could listen in on the interview. Chris was pleasant and respectful, but he had little to say for himself or his project.

The judge was patient and kind, trying to draw Chris out. But Chris responded to each question with a small smile and a nod or shake of the head. He was not a talker.

Clearly mystified as to the purpose of the exhibit, the judge finally asked outright, "What exactly will you use this thing for?"

"It's for skateboarding," Chris said.

"What do you mean?"

"It's for a skateboard. You set it up on a hard surface, like a sidewalk. Then you build up some speed and ollie off it," Chris explained. "You can get some pretty big air." Chris said nothing about the design or engineering aspects of his project: the carefully calculated degree of slope and transition, angle of approach, or ratio of rise to run.

"Sounds kind of dangerous." The judge frowned as he studied the ramp. Asking a few more questions, the man gave Chris every opportunity to explain its significance. Chris responded only with a shy smile, a shrug of the shoulders, or a simple yes or no. Looking defeated, the judge searched for something positive to say to the boy with the gruesome project.

A long line of kids had formed behind Chris, and the judge knew he had to move on. There was nothing else he could do. He reached into a box of ribbons and handed Chris a white one. He offered Chris a few tips on how to improve his work for next year. The judge said, "You can't make a silk purse out of a sow's ear." He suggested using a higher quality material, like maple or oak, instead of plywood. Something you could sand and varnish. Something you could display in the living room of your home to be admired for years to come.

The interview was over, and Chris's project had received the lowest possible rating. Though he was disappointed, he thanked the judge for his time and advice. Chris scanned the crowd and spotted me, standing beside a table of small wooden clocks, all bearing blue ribbons.

Chris made his way toward me, dodging harried mothers carrying boxes of craft projects. Already, his good-natured swagger was back in place. His face broke into its familiar dimpled grin; he shrugged his shoulders one last time and said, "Guess I should have varnished it."

There was no sign of a bruised ego or damaged self-esteem. He was still our extraordinary boy of eternal optimism, quiet self-assurance, unsophisticated flair and grace. For Chris, the beauty and utility of a project was in its function, not its appearance. The hulking slab of plywood and iron sitting in the exhibit hall was merely the scaffolding, like the pieces of a NASA launching pad that fall away when a rocket lifts off. The real project was something else entirely. If that ugly old sow's ear had just the right combination of strength, stability, and proportion, Chris knew he would gain something far better than a blue ribbon. He would fly.

✳

Chris also enrolled in the 4-H cat show every year. For this event, each participant may enter both a cat and an educational poster. The judge examines each cat for health and condition, then asks the exhibitor a series of questions on cat care, cat anatomy, cat diseases, and anything else one might possibly want to know about a cat. The children are judged on their knowledge as well as the cleanliness and condition of the cat being exhibited.

Chris never did too well in the interview part, because that would have required some study and preparation. He was already on the receiving end of an education—courtesy of the State of Minnesota—that consumed nine months of his year, and he didn't want to spend any extra time on educational pursuits in the summer months. His policy was to just show up and hope for the best.

About twenty minutes before the show was to begin, Chris grabbed one of the cats that lay snoring in the castle. He could usually get a cat stuffed into the carrier before it woke up completely and realized what was happening. This may explain why the cat always burst so angrily out of the carrier when it was opened on the judge's table at the fairgrounds.

That year, Mr. Tinkles was the unlucky passenger. Snarls, hisses, and angry howls emanated from the carrier as Mr. Tinkles traveled the seven miles to the fairgrounds in the car. We arrived just in time, as Chris was being called to the judge's table.

Mr. Tinkles is not a docile pet at the best of times, and he had been pushed to his limit by being forced into the carrier and hauled away while still half asleep. The indignity was just too much, and when Chris opened the carrier door, Tinkles sprang out and sank his claws and teeth into the first thing he encountered. The judge.

The judge's assistants managed to extricate Tinkles's teeth and claws from the woman's shoulder and chest with a minimum of bloodshed. Showing remarkable restraint, the judge turned to Chris and suggested that his cat remain in its carrier for the rest of the show. Mr. Tinkles was the only cat to participate in the show while behind bars.

After Chris's turn at the judge's table, he carried the disgraced Mr. Tinkles, still confined to his cage, to the bench where Terry and I sat in the bleachers. The judge followed Chris's progress with her eyes, and my face burned with embarrassment when she aimed a stern glare at Terry and me.

Immediately following the cat show was the poster contest. Mr. Tinkles scowled in his cage while Chris carried his poster to the judging table. The other children had made posters with titles such as *Common Diseases of the Housecat* or *Anatomy of the Domestic Shorthair.* Mindful of Mr. Tinkles's unpredictable temperament, Chris had made a poster titled *How to Treat a Cat Bite.* I'm sure the judge found the exhibit both helpful and enlightening.

During the week of the county fair, Chris was busy showing rabbits and sheep. At that time there were no classes for those of the camelid persuasion, so Tony the alpaca was entered in the 4-H pet show.

On the evening of the pet show, we cajoled and petted Tony, trying to convince him to climb the ramp of the livestock trailer. Finally, with a bucket of grain to entice him, Tony entered the trailer. Tony was not happy at being dragged away from his grazing, and he sulked in the trailer and refused to come out when we reached the fairgrounds. But before long, Tony's curiosity got the best of him. He could hear and smell all kinds of interesting things, and soon he stepped out of the trailer and allowed Chris to lead him to the show arena.

Tony hummed excitedly, and he swiveled his head in all directions to take in the sights. When Chris and Tony reached the arena, Chris paused to scan the day's agenda and list of entries posted by the door. After studying the list, Chris was confident he and Tony would do well at the pet show. He might even have a shot at first place. The other entrants were a goldfish, a hamster, a parakeet, a snail, and a mouse. How could any of those pets begin to compare to the large and exotic Tony, who stood batting his long eyelashes at the judge? Tony leaned toward the official-looking woman in the white lab coat and inquired politely, "Hmmmm?"

Each participant spent about ten minutes alone with the judge, showing their pets and explaining their care. By this time, even Terry and I were quite sure Chris and Tony would do well in the competition. I couldn't imagine what anyone could possibly have to say about a snail or a goldfish.

When the interviews were finished, the judge picked up the microphone to announce the results. We sat in the bleachers and beamed down at Chris, who stood expectantly beside Tony. After naming the reserve champion, the judge shuffled through her notes and prepared to announce the winner of the class. She turned toward the audience and said, "Congratulations to Ben Larson and his pet mouse!"

Terry, Chris, and I were stunned. How could the judge have overlooked Tony and awarded the first prize to a mouse?

The judge praised Ben for his extensive knowledge on the husbandry of the mouse. Apparently the boy could recite the diseases of the rodent in vivid detail. He knew exactly how to care for the small creature, and he excelled at the interview portion of the competition. I couldn't help but notice the jar was indeed spotless, and it was obvious the mouse was well fed, well groomed, and well cared for.

I glanced over at Chris and Tony. Chris had absolutely no desire to discuss the gestation period or obscure diseases of the South American ruminant. And then there was Tony, who—though extremely polite—still had stray wisps of straw clinging to his cowlick, and his dreadful teeth needed a good cleaning. His deranged geisha girl look didn't speak well for Chris's diligence in the care and grooming department. Maybe the judge had made the right call after all.

※

Finally it was Friday, and Chris's last event was the lamb lead. Sponsored by the Minnesota Wool Producers, this event is a competition in which the children lead their lambs around the arena while modeling clothing made from wool.

Chris enters the lamb lead every year. And every year, Chris is beaten by a girl. The same girl has been named grand champion of the junior lamb lead for as long as I can remember, and she deserves the honor. She has spent her summer working with her lamb, grooming it for show, and stitching her woolen garment—unlike Chris, who had spent his summer biking, skateboarding, watching television game shows, and perfecting his fart imitation, using only one small plastic straw and his armpit.

On the morning of the lamb lead, the sky was overcast and threatening. We hadn't had any rain in nearly a month, and everyone hoped the dark clouds would deliver a soaker. I heard thunder roll in the distance as I rushed into the arena to find a seat. We really needed the moisture, but I hoped the cloudburst would wait until Chris and Lamb Chop made it into the show ring.

Terry and Chris were still in the sheep exhibition barn, where Lamb Chop and a few of our other sheep had spent the week. Terry was helping Chris get Lamb Chop into her show halter and Chris himself get into the woolen sweater vest I had knit especially for this occasion, using bulky homespun yarn from our own flock. I thought the simplicity of the garment was an appropriate complement to the primitive sheep breed that Chris was showing.

Chris's sheep and woolen vest were a far cry from those of the rest of the exhibitors. Almost all of the other children showed large market lambs that were neatly shorn for the event. The wool breeds of sheep, such as Shetland and Icelandic, are much smaller and are traditionally shown with a full coat of wool. Naturally, they look a bit ragged beside the shaved Dorsets and Hampshires. The other children wore clothing sewn from lightweight woolen fabrics, and none but Chris wore knitted sweaters. After all, it was August.

Seated on the wooden bleachers, I craned my neck so I could see the expanse of bare ground between the exhibition barns and the show arena. I watched and waited for Chris and Lamb Chop to appear.

Finally they emerged from the barn. Chris tugged mightily on the lead rope, and Lamb Chop stubbornly held her ground. When Chris had managed to drag her halfway to the arena, the skies opened and a deluge of rain drenched the two struggling figures. Chris pulled hard, but Lamb Chop planted her front hooves firmly in the dust, refusing to budge.

The other exhibitors were already lined up in the show ring. Chris and Lamb Chop were late. At last, they stumbled into the arena. Chris was soaking wet, his hair plastered to his head and his sodden oversized sweater—I made it big enough to last for several years—stretching nearly to his knees.

Lamb Chop stood dripping beside him, bleating unhappily. They looked like something that might have washed up on the beach of a remote Scottish isle. You could almost hear the bagpipes and smell the peat smoke.

Chris and Lamb Chop took their place at the end of the line and waited for the judging to begin. In this event, the children are judged not only on the appearance of their lamb and their woolen garment but on their knowledge of the wool industry. In previous years the judge had asked technical questions such as, "How many microns of wool are there to a square inch of fabric?" These were the types of questions with which Chris struggled. The girl who always won the lamb lead had ready answers.

But this year, the judge took a different approach. He questioned the exhibitors on their knowledge of wool processing—from shearing the sheep to washing the wool to carding, drying, spinning, and weaving it. Chris was in his element, since he had either done these tasks himself or watched as Terry and I did them. He perked up a little during the judge's questioning. But I knew Chris had no illusions about earning the grand champion ribbon or the trophy that went with it. He would be more than happy to land a blue ribbon, which came with a twelve-dollar cash prize.

The judge finished his questions, and then he stepped back to look over the exhibitors and their lambs one last time. He asked the children to circle the arena, leading their lambs.

The girl who always won the competition stepped out confidently with her well-behaved lamb by her side. Following the proper showmanship guidelines, she maintained eye contact with the judge and kept her lamb between herself and the judge at all times. One by one, the other exhibitors joined in, leading their lambs around the circle. Chris was last in line, and when he tugged on Lamb Chop's lead rope, she simply sighed and lay down.

The audience broke into loud laughter. The other exhibitors finished circling the arena and had returned to their places in line by the time Chris was able to prod the stubborn Lamb Chop to her feet.

The judge stepped to the microphone and cleared his throat. He made the usual announcements, thanking the Minnesota Wool Producers for donating the trophy and prize money. He thanked the 4-H clubs and parents for their support and encouragement, then explained the judging standards of the lamb lead in great detail. Finally, he was ready to award the trophy and ribbons.

First came the reserve champion. Terry and I were not surprised when our son was bypassed for this honor. He and Lamb Chop looked pitiful. Both were dripping wet, and by now Lamb Chop was also covered in dust from her roll on the arena's dirt floor.

Then the judge continued, "This year the grand champion of the junior lamb lead is Christopher Sletto." Chris looked up in amazement at Terry and me where we sat in the stands, our jaws hanging open in shock.

Terry leaned over to me and whispered, "There must be some mistake. He can't have won it."

The judge said, "Though some of the other exhibitors may have shown their garments and animals in a less . . ." He paused, clearly searching for a phrase that didn't include the words sloppy, shaggy, or unkempt. ". . . primitive manner, this young man certainly knows his wool processing."

The Douglas County Fair was over, and Chris, armed with his prize money, convinced Terry to stop at Fleet Farm on the way home.

Mack Dawg's very bad day

Our scheme to turn Mack Dawg into a guard llama was not exactly working out as planned. After the mating of Mack and Camilla, we moved Mack to the sheep pasture to bond with the flock, while Camilla was temporarily penned separately in the adjacent pasture. But Mack had no desire to bond with sheep. He wanted Camilla. He spent all of his waking hours pacing along the fence line that separated him from his long-haired, snaggle-toothed paramour. He remained totally oblivious to the sheep grazing nearby in his quest to rejoin Camilla.

On those rare occasions when we coaxed him away from his vigil, he was playful and friendly with Terry, Chris, and me. He especially liked to chase Chris around the pasture. When we had friends over, I encouraged Chris to go in the pen and run with the llama as entertainment for our guests. And it was genuinely entertaining. Like Tigger in the *Winnie-the-Pooh* stories, Mack loved to bounce. He bounced on and over everything in his path—people, pets, and other livestock included.

But over time, Mack's bouncing games grew rougher and more aggressive. After being knocked over a few times ourselves, we no longer found his bouncing very funny. Finally, we moved Mack into an isolated pen out of sight of the sheep pasture, so we wouldn't have to deal with his rough behavior every time we fed or worked with the sheep. We returned Camilla to the sheep pasture, hoping that a complete separation from Camilla might calm Mack down.

I called Iris, his previous owner, and asked if she and George had any idea what could be causing Mack's odd behavior. They were as bewildered as we were. Another friend suggested we contact the county extension office: they might have some information on the matter. Of course, I thought. Extension had been invaluable when we had questions on various other livestock topics. So the next morning I arrived bright and early at the extension office.

"Do you have any information on llama behavioral problems?" I asked the woman at the front desk.

She raised her eyebrows, looked blankly at me, and asked, "What?"

"Llamas. Do you have any information on llamas?"

"We don't get much call for that type of thing here in Douglas County," she said. She was too polite to say what was really on her mind: "Why would any sane person want to raise llamas?"

After an Internet search yielded no useful information, I decided to try my luck at the public library. Searching through the computerized card catalog, I found several items listed under llamas. All were either texts on South American wildlife or children's picture books. One of those, *Fluffy the Friendly Llama,* caught my eye. Had it been titled *Fluffy the Demented Llama* or *Fluffy the Killer Llama* I might have made an effort to locate it. I was disappointed to find nothing resembling a reference book on coping with aggressive llamas.

But the research librarian thought something might be available through interlibrary loan. She made a few quick entries on her computer and came up with an encyclopedia on llama care and breeding. "I can order it from the library in Morris, and it'll be here in about a week," she said.

Meanwhile, solitary confinement had not lessened Mack's fixation. He spent most of his day pacing up and down the fence line, still yearning for Camilla.

After three days of isolation, it seemed Mack had endured enough solitude. Terry, Chris, and I were all away from home when Mack made his escape. How he accomplished it is still a mystery.

Returning home that afternoon, I turned into our driveway and was surprised to see no sheep grazing in the far pasture, their usual afternoon spot. As I continued up the driveway, I could see no sheep grazing along the road in the lower pasture, and no sheep standing in the sheep yard. I couldn't imagine where the flock could be hiding.

When I pulled into the yard, I saw Mack Dawg lying triumphantly on top of a mound of dirt just outside the sheep shed door. He had somehow jumped the fence of his pen. And instead of making a break for freedom once he was loose, he jumped another impossibly high fence into the pasture with Camilla and the other livestock.

Realizing Mack and Camilla were once again in the same vicinity, I imagined the reunion of the two lovesick llamas must have been a highly charged emotional event. But by the time I arrived, Mack didn't seem the least bit interested in reviving his flame of passion with Camilla. No romantic tryst this time: it seemed Mack had made the monumental effort of jumping two fences for the sole purpose of taunting Camilla and the other occupants of the pasture.

Mack had apparently spent his afternoon rounding them up and was now holding them captive in the sheep shed. He lay on the mound of dirt outside the door, carefully monitoring their movements. All of the sheep and Tony the alpaca were cowering at the back of the shed in fear of the big brown bully. Only Camilla and Rosie periodically stuck their heads out the open shed door to glare at Mack. It was the height of their afternoon grazing time, and the animals were not pleased at being trapped in the hot, airless shed.

Camilla, her ears laid back against her head, once again poked her head out to stare angrily at Mack. He responded with a casual sidelong glance over his shoulder and a loud snort. Camilla jerked her head back into the shed after aiming a vile spray of grass-stained spittle in Mack's direction. Clearly there had been a lovers' spat, and the entire flock was suffering the consequences.

The standoff ended when Terry got home. He lured Mack away from his post with a bucket of grain and returned him to his pen without incident. The other animals stepped out of the shed, looking cautiously about, hoping the terrorist was gone. When they realized Mack was nowhere in sight, they galloped off to resume their grazing.

About a week later the llama reference book arrived at the library. I picked it up and rushed home to research Mack's strange affliction. I paged quickly through chapters on the care, breeding, diet, diseases, and training of llamas. Finally, at the back of the book I found a chapter titled "Llamas Behaving Badly." It described a behavioral condition that fit Mack exactly: berserk male syndrome.

This honest-to-goodness condition affects a small percentage of male llamas. Berserk male syndrome is a behavioral disorder, characterized by excessive aggression toward humans and other llamas. A llama in the throes of berserk male syndrome chest-bumps people and other llamas roughly, often knocking them down. He may also bite viciously or wrestle his victims to the ground.

This rare condition usually affects llamas who have been bottle-fed or excessively handled by humans when they were young. Abnormally socialized, these llamas see humans not as their masters, but rather as creatures equivalent to the other llamas in the herd. When the afflicted llama's reproductive hormones kick in—as did Mack's when he met Camilla—he becomes protective and attempts to drive everyone, humans and animals alike, out of his territory and away from his mate.

Though the book described Mack's condition, there was no mention of a treatment or cure. It did have an index of authorities on various topics who could be contacted with questions. I picked up the phone and dialed the number of the man who was listed as the llama behavioral expert.

The man listened to my description of Mack's symptoms, and he confirmed the diagnosis I already suspected. Mack Dawg was most certainly afflicted with berserk male syndrome.

"Is there any cure?" I asked.

The expert didn't mince words. He replied, "There are only two known remedies. One involves castration and the other a loaded rifle."

I reported this news to Terry, and we agreed. Mack Dawg was dangerous and would have to be castrated as soon as possible. We made an appointment with Dan, our vet, for the following day.

❋

We asked Dan to arrive after three o'clock that afternoon to castrate Mack. Terry would be home from work by then, and I'd be through with my business meeting: I was discussing an affordable housing project with city, county, and state agency representatives in a nearby town. But we knew that because of the nature of Dan's work, his schedule was often erratic. From past experience we knew he could arrive much earlier or much later than expected.

Large-animal vets like Dan usually make their rounds of farm calls alone, and it's expected that the farmer will have lined up assistance to catch and subdue the animal to be treated. But every vet can tell stories about clients who haven't made those arrangements, and the vet arrives only to find that he must single-handedly locate and capture his half-ton patient before he can even think of making a diagnosis and administering treatment—which explains why the vet's schedule is so erratic.

That day, I kept my cell phone at hand during my meeting, contrary to my usual practice. At that early point in my career, I was still trying to maintain the illusion of professionalism. I wanted my clients to think I ran a normal consulting business out of a legitimate office. But this time I apologized in advance for the phone call I might need to take during the meeting, explaining that a situation had arisen at my office, and a colleague might call. I didn't mention the colleague was a twelve-year-old child, nor that the situation involved the castration of a berserk llama.

Since Chris was home alone, I was worried that he might try to catch and handle Mack by himself if Dan arrived early to do the castration. Mack was unpredictable at the best of times, and I didn't want to risk Chris's safety. I told Chris to call me on my cell phone if Dan arrived before Terry or I got home that afternoon.

I sincerely hoped the phone wouldn't ring until my meeting was over. But in the middle of the meeting and a full hour before we expected Dan to arrive, my cell phone rang.

"Hello?" I turned away from the conference table and answered in a whisper, trying not to disturb the discussion.

On the other end of the line the voice of Christopher said, "Dan's here. He wants to get started with the llama right away. He's got a lot of other stops to make today."

I turned back to the group and said, "Something's come up back at the office, and I'm going to have to leave early."

Then, speaking into the phone, I said to Chris, "Stall him, and I'll get there as soon as I can."

The others in the meeting looked at me with concern, and the man beside me said, "I hope everything's all right at your office?"

"Everything's fine," I said as I turned my attention back to the phone, hoping to cut the conversation short. But Chris was not that easily put off.

"What should I tell him?" Chris persisted.

"Umm . . . Have him take a look at that lump on the dog's back." I tried to think of some benign activity to keep the vet distracted until I could get there.

"What lump on which dog?" Chris asked.

There was a lull in the conversation in the conference room, and the others were beginning to give me strange looks. I turned my back to the group and tried to speak more quietly. "I don't know!" I hissed into the phone. "There must be lumps on at least one of those dogs! Or how about that ingrown horn on the black ram lamb? Just stall for time until I get there."

"Dad already took care of the ingrown horn."

"Well . . . Have Dan treat that old angora buck for wool block."

"Okay," Chris said as he hung up the phone.

I turned back to the group at the conference table, and one of the state agency people said, "Where's your office? At the zoo?"

That got a laugh from the entire group. I made a flimsy excuse and left the meeting.

Terry arrived home just as I did, and Dan was ready to start on Mack Dawg's procedure. He gathered the surgical instruments from the back of his truck, and we joined him outside Mack's pen.

During the weeks of Mack's rampaging episodes, his wool and toenails had grown very long. Neither Terry nor I had any desire to climb the fence and pare the toenails of a llama gone berserk. So when we learned Dan planned to put Mack under with general anesthesia for the castration, we figured it was the perfect opportunity to shear his wool and cut his nails.

Mack was alert and curious about all the activity outside of his pen. He leaned against the fence with his head stretched over the top wire to get a good view of the situation. An exhausting and dangerous chase wouldn't be necessary. Dan reached easily over the fence and gave Mack a tranquilizing injection in his shoulder.

The anesthesia took effect almost immediately. Mack began weaving crazily around the pen. He tried to run, but his knees buckled. After making a few loopy circles around the pasture, Mack gave in to the overwhelming sensation. He toppled over and fell to the ground.

Time was of the essence, since Dan guessed Mack would stay unconscious for only about twenty minutes. Dan, Terry, Chris, and I climbed over the fence and rushed to the prone figure, tools in hand. Chris was reluctant to get involved with the grisly project, but we would need every pair of hands available to finish all the tasks while Mack was asleep.

We had agreed upon a plan of action in advance. Chris and I would shear Mack's wool using manual sheep shears. Terry would trim Mack's toenails while Dan did the castration. We had to work fast, and each of us bent to our assigned task as soon as Mack hit the ground.

Dan quickly realized that he needed someone's help to hold Mack's hind leg up so that he could get at the llama's scrotum. "Hey, Chris, could you give me a hand over here?"

Chris put down his shears and moved to assist Dan.

"Here, buddy. Can you just hoist up this hind leg and hold it out of the way so I can do the cutting?" asked Dan.

Looking slightly queasy, Chris turned his head away to avoid seeing the scalpel at work. Dan said, "Chris! You need to keep your eye on what I'm doing here. You've got to keep repositioning the leg so I have a clear view of the incision at all times."

Helplessly, Chris watched, adjusting the leg when necessary, as Dan expertly incised the flesh and removed the llama's testicles. Chris's pallor intensified when a hurried and distracted Dan tossed the small round objects directly over Chris's shoulder, narrowly missing his left ear. The dogs, never far from the action, pounced upon these delicacies and devoured them instantly.

Terry finished trimming Mack's toenails and moved to help me with the shearing. By the time we were done, Mack was awake and struggling to his feet. We led him to a small pen beside the sheep pasture where he could recover in clean, grassy surroundings.

Even though Mack managed to stand, he was still unsteady on his feet. He staggered pathetically about the pen, feeling very sorry for himself. Just minutes earlier—before the procedure began—he was a cocky, self-assured rascal. Mack had always been vain, and he was proud of his appearance. But now, after his extreme makeover, Mack was a very sad and sorry individual. He sought out Camilla, hoping she would offer him comfort. During the procedure, Camilla had remained nearby on her side of the fence, watching the proceedings with interest. But when Mack hobbled up beside her, Camilla took one long look at him before spitting scornfully in his face and galloping away.

Camilla didn't recognize him. Mack's majestic coat of wool was gone. He minced along on his freshly cropped toenails, and he smelled of antiseptic. This was not the splendid mate she remembered.

Castration marked the end of an era for Mack. Gone was the virile, studly rogue of his glory days, when he had terrorized the entire neighborhood with his antics. Though we knew he had been a dangerous animal before his surgery, we regretted having to reduce him to this state.

September

L amb Chop returned home in triumph from the county fair, having basked in the attention she received as grand champion. At the same time, we had some serious concerns about Lamb Chop's future. Fall was just around the corner, and winter wasn't far behind. For her own safety, Lamb Chop would need to stay in the pasture and shed with the other sheep when winter came. She couldn't continue to spend her days sleeping on the lawn and chasing cars with the dogs for much longer.

By mid-September one of the problems had resolved itself. Lamb Chop grew too big to squeeze through the gaps in the fence, so she could no longer escape from the shed or pasture.

Chris's summer vacation ended and he returned to school, leaving Lamb Chop feeling lonely and neglected. He no longer came to the shed or pasture each morning to fetch Lamb Chop for the day's activities. During this time she stood for hours at the pasture gate, bleating sadly and gazing wistfully at the house.

One day in mid-September, as I sped down the driveway on my way to town, the dogs embarked on their ferocious pursuit of my car. Inside the fence, Lamb Chop ran along beside Petey and Bart, trying hard to keep up her part in the old game.

The pasture ended a good fifty yards before the end of the driveway, and Lamb Chop was forced to halt abruptly while the dogs continued their run. Lamb Chop stood dejected, her face pushed through the wire netting of the fence, watching the dogs complete the chase. When Petey and Bart reached the approach to the county highway, they turned and trotted back to the farm. Lamb Chop bleated excitedly, hoping for an acknowledgment from her old friends. But the dogs seemed to have forgotten her, ignoring her as they passed by. Again, I was haunted by Terry's prediction, "You won't be doing her a favor by making a pet of her."

※

Whiplash was integrating well into the flock. Though she was tame and friendly, she never became as dependent upon humans as Lamb Chop did. She would be fine.

Bottle lambs are usually smaller and less hardy than those fed by their mothers. But Whiplash had a secret advantage. By the time she was a few months old, she had caught up in size to the rest of the spring lambs, thanks mainly to her night raids on the unguarded udders in the sheep shed.

※

Like Lamb Chop and Whiplash, Rambling Rose was growing. She was still only half the size of the other spring lambs, but we were surprised at how well she was managing. She became skilled at tracking her mother's location, thanks to the bell. Rambling Rose stuck close to Rosie and learned to graze with the flock. She was holding her own, and it seemed things might finally be looking up for Rambling Rose.

Still, we were constantly alert to the coyote danger. We saw them, usually at dusk, loping down the dirt road or crossing the hayfield on their way to drink at the lake. The increased savagery of the coyotes that summer made everyone uneasy.

❀

The ad for Buck appeared in the September issue of the sheep breeders' magazine. A few days later, I got a call from a prospective buyer. David Lewis from Michigan had obviously spent some time researching the pedigrees of Shetland sheep in general and Rosie and Lloyd in particular. Mr. Lewis wanted to buy Buck, and he had some impressive plans for the young ram. He was involved in breeding and showing Shetlands nationally, and he was looking for some new blood with good show prospects.

"I've done some checking on that lineage. If that lamb turns out to be half the ram I think he'll be, you're going to have people beating down your door to buy breeding stock," said Mr. Lewis. "I hope you've got plenty more young rams and ewes to sell, because there's going to be a demand for them once the word gets out."

I felt myself swell with pride, and I couldn't wait to tell Terry the good news. When I heard Terry's truck drive into the yard that afternoon, I rushed outside to meet him. Our goal of becoming serious contenders in the registered Shetland sheep market was within reach.

As Terry got out of his truck, I launched into the tale, concluding with Mr. Lewis's prediction of our future success. "All we've got to do now is schedule the vet check and get all the vaccinations so we can transport Buck across state lines."

Terry replied, "Hmm."

"What! That's all you've got to say? I've finally gotten some results in marketing the breeding stock, and that's all you've got to say?" I was outraged by his apathy. "This could be huge!

We could be selling champion breeding stock across the country once Buck gets established in Michigan. This could be the one thing that makes our whole operation financially viable!"

Terry stood in silence, looking out over the flock grazing in the lower pasture. Then he turned to me and said, "What if Rambling Rose's problems are genetic?"

He let the implications sink in before he continued. "We can't in good conscience sell her twin as a breeding ram, can we? Buck is carrying the same genes Rambling Rose is."

"I thought Rose's problems were caused by oxygen deprivation at birth," I said.

"Let me show you something," Terry said as he led the way into the house. He pulled out the dog-eared flock record book, and he flipped to the back where we had recorded all the lamb births over the past four years.

Terry pointed to the page where the details of Rosie's first lambing were written. "Set of twins," he read aloud. "Healthy moorit male. Frail white ewe lamb, lacking coordination. Ewe lamb died at one day of age."

Thinking back, I remembered the white lamb mentioned in the notes. All at once it came back to me: the odd tilt of the head, the lack of coordination, and the general failure to thrive, all evident even on her first day of life. It was frighteningly similar to Rambling Rose's early characteristics, minus the rambling.

"Why didn't we think of this sooner?" I asked Terry. "The similarities seem so obvious now, but it never occurred to me before."

"It was Rosie's first lambing. We just assumed the problems were caused by her inexperience." Terry said. "Remember? The white ewe lamb wasn't even totally out of the placenta when we found her, and we figured it was birth trauma or oxygen deprivation. Never anything congenital. But Rambling Rose could hardly have experienced birth trauma or oxygen deprivation. Both twins were born in the time it took you to walk out to get the mail."

I paged through the notebook, stunned. None of the other lambs born on our farm over the past four years had been afflicted with anything similar. No trace of problems in any of Rosie's other lambs, or Ada's, either.

"I just started thinking about the genetics in the last week or so," Terry said. "Then I looked back at the records, and it all seemed to fall into place. We had already placed the ad in the journal."

My heart sank as I thought of the prospective sale of Buck. So many hopes and dreams down the drain. I was so confident that Buck was the ticket to our future as legitimate Shetland sheep breeders. The successful launching of Buck could have been the key factor in my ability to return to full-time shepherding.

"We've got to do the right thing," Terry said before he headed outside to start the evening chores.

-❋-

I picked up the phone and called David Lewis in Michigan. I told him that the sale of the ram lamb was off.

"What happened?" Mr. Lewis was surprised and angry. "Did you get a better offer?"

"The lamb is no longer for sale," I repeated.

"Damn it! I had my heart set on that little moorit!" Mr. Lewis wasn't about to drop the matter so easily. "What if I raise my price?"

It was hard to reply, knowing how much the sale would mean to the financial future of our flock and my dream of full-time shepherding. My resolve to break the deal wavered. After all, it was only speculation that Buck had genetic issues. He could be perfectly sound. Maybe Terry was being too cautious.

After a long pause, I replied. "Sorry. No."

Steve, the wayward rabbit

One day I got a phone call from a woman who heard through the grapevine that I raised angora rabbits. "Do you want five more?" she asked. "We bought a whole litter of baby angoras last spring, and we need to find homes for them before winter."

She explained her predicament. She and her family lived on a farm near the small town of Starbuck. Her eight-year-old daughter Stephanie was a member of the local 4-H club. "Stephanie somehow got it in her head that—more than anything else in the world—she wanted angora rabbits to raise and show for 4-H. So we bought a litter of angora babies last spring."

Stephanie dived wholeheartedly into her new rabbit project. But as the days and weeks passed, Stephanie and her family learned angoras weren't as easy to care for as they thought. By September, the cute bunnies had grown into five tangled and matted adults. Angoras require extra grooming to keep them from becoming a snarled mess. Stephanie couldn't manage it by herself. Her dad was busy with work, and her mother discovered she was allergic to angora wool.

Hence the anxious phone call. I knew I shouldn't take on any more rabbits. I had started out with three angoras, and slowly and insidiously, that number had grown. At that time I owned nearly forty rabbits. In addition to the angoras I raised for wool, we housed seven miscellaneous non-wool-bearing hangers-on, who had worn out their welcome at their previous homes and were living out their days on our farm.

From a very modest beginning in a corner of Terry's hay shed, my rabbitry expanded to take over the entire upper floor of the shed, and it was fast encroaching on the lower half, which housed the sheep. I certainly did not need another five rabbits.

I tried my best to boldly say no to the woman's offer, but I just couldn't force the word out. As luck would have it, I did have one empty cage. One of my oldest angoras had just died. I told the woman, "I can't promise anything, but I can come over and take a look. I have room for one rabbit, and I could probably use a new buck."

Terry was working in the garage when I was ready to leave that afternoon. I told him where I was headed, and without a word he wiped the grease off his hands and slid behind the wheel of the truck.

"Are you interested in looking at rabbits?" I asked in surprise.

"Yeah," he said. "It'll probably improve the odds of you coming home with only one rabbit, and not five."

Twenty minutes later we drove into the farmyard and were greeted by Stephanie and her dad, Curt. We managed to introduce ourselves to Curt, but that was all we could do before Stephanie began her enthusiastic sales pitch.

"You're here to buy some rabbits, huh? Well, I've got a real good deal for you. Two for the price of one. Or all five for the price of three. Take your pick. They're real big and healthy except for the ear mites. Hey! Don't step on that cat! Come on. This way. I'll show you the rabbits. Did I tell you they're on sale today?"

Stephanie could have launched a career as a carnival barker or an auctioneer, given her gregarious nature and the fluid rapidity of her speech.

The rabbits were housed in cages inside a horse stall in the barn. Dozens of cats and kittens appeared out of nowhere, climbing over the tops of the cages and squeezing everywhere in between. Stephanie's nonstop commentary provided pleasant background chatter as I examined the five rabbits. Their wool was certainly tangled and matted, but they were well cared for and healthy, with no sign of mites or other parasites.

I liked the look of one of the bucks in particular, and I asked Stephanie if she was willing to part with him. "You bet," she said. "I'll throw a couple of cats in on the deal," she added, shaking my hand to seal the bargain.

While Terry and Curt loaded the rabbit and its traveling cage into the back of the pickup, I bent down to pat the head of an old dog that had been trailing along behind us. "What's his name?" I asked Stephanie.

"Toby," said Stephanie. "Do you like dogs?"

"Yes, I sure do," I answered.

"Well, for five bucks you've got yourself a dog." Stephanie hefted the fat, sagging hound into the back of the truck and was about to slam the tailgate shut when her dad returned.

"Hey, wait a minute!" Curt laughed as he pulled the old hound out of the truck. "This is the Nelsons' dog. He's not even ours. You know better than to sell him, Steph," he scolded.

Terry and I got into the truck. Before we reached the end of the driveway, we both burst out laughing at the spunk and sheer audacity of the girl. She had totally made our day.

When the laughter subsided, I said, "Oh, we forgot to ask what the rabbit's name is."

"Stephanie," said Terry. "Let's call it Stephanie."

"There's just one problem," I replied. "It's a male rabbit."

After a moment's thought Terry said, "Well, how about Steve?"

"Okay. Steve it is."

When we arrived home, I carried Steve to the rabbit shed and settled him in the empty cage. I filled the feeders with water, hay, and the rabbits' grain mixture. It was then I remembered the latch was broken, and the door to the cage hung loose from one hinge. This hadn't mattered for the cage's previous occupant, who, in her fading golden years, sat placidly in the cage, even though the door hung open at all times.

But Steve was an entirely different story. He was young and active. I tied a neat bow with a length of baler twine to secure the door, and then I went in search of materials to make more permanent repairs to the cage.

Just then, Chris appeared outside the house, calling, "Mom! Phone call."

"Get a number, and I'll call back later," I yelled from the shed door.

"I think you should take it. It's the third time this lady has called since you left. She says it's important."

Chris's phone-answering and message-taking skills were really improving, I thought as I hurried to the house to take the call. I took the wireless phone from Chris at the door. "Hello?" I said, entering the house and heading toward the living room, where I could sit down and take notes.

The call was from the clerk of Norcross, a small town about fifty miles west of our farm. The city council members had heard about my work on a housing rehabilitation program in nearby Herman, and they wondered if something similar could be done in their town. "We've got a city council meeting tonight," the clerk told me. "I don't suppose you could come at eight o'clock and give us some information?"

Halfway across the living room, as I passed the antique dresser, I realized I hadn't looked up to see if Luigi was hiding there. It was too late.

"Yeow!" I screamed directly into the phone as Luigi landed on my shoulders. His claws dug savagely into my back and neck as he tried to maintain his precarious balance on his moving target.

"Pardon me?" responded the clerk. "What did you say?"

Silently cursing the darn cat, I grabbed the scruff of Luigi's neck, ripped him off my back, and flung him onto the couch. "*Reeeeerrrrr!*" Luigi screamed as he thudded against the soft cushions and then bounced to the floor. He scampered away with a flourish of his black tail.

"Serves you right!" I mouthed silently but emphatically to the cat.

I returned my attention back to the telephone. "Yes. Yeow! I'm just so excited about this project. I'll see you in a couple of hours."

※

I was happy at the prospect of another consulting job, but I was also reminded of the neglected items on my shepherdess to-do list. Fall was rapidly approaching and I still hadn't registered our flock for any of the Shetland sheep shows. After the sale of Buck fell through, I just didn't have the heart to expend more effort on marketing the breeding stock.

After preparing for the city council meeting, I drove the hour to Norcross, where I landed another grant writing job. Steve and his faulty cage door were forgotten.

The next morning I went out early to check the animals. Steve was looking a little lost and confused, but he was still in his cage. He hadn't chewed through the baler twine, but he'd eaten all of the hay and most of the grain mixture I left him the previous afternoon. He seemed to be adjusting to his new environment.

"It looks like that'll hold you for awhile." I said to Steve. "I don't have time to fix your cage right now. But we've got to cut your hair soon. I've never seen such a mess!"

Steve averted his eyes and his face took on a guilty, remorseful look.

"Oh, don't feel so bad," I said. "You take things way too seriously."

And he did seem to be a very serious, solemn individual. He wasn't at all playful, like the other young rabbits. He wore a quizzical, worried expression on his whiskered face at all times.

Later that afternoon I was carrying buckets of water to the animals when Terry drove into the yard. He rolled down the truck window and said, "Look what I found on my way home from work." He leaned over and swung open the passenger door. I walked around to see.

It was Steve, sitting on the seat beside Terry.

"What? It's Steve! Where did you find him?"

"I saw something hairy in the road ditch, heading south. When I pulled up alongside, I realized it was Steve. Looked like he was on his way back to Starbuck," said Terry.

"What were you thinking?" I demanded of Steve. "You could have been killed out there on the highway!" Steve's perplexed look was replaced by one of remorse, and he turned his head and refused to make eye contact.

I carried Steve back to his cage in the shed. Sure enough, the baler twine had been chewed through, and the cage door hung open. I put Steve back in and wove two strands of baler twine through the wires to hold the door firmly shut. I would have to finish my llama chores before making a more permanent fix to the door.

"And, don't forget, we still need to cut your hair and toenails," I reminded Steve.

But somehow the remaining hours of that day just slipped away. I was busy with one vital task after another, and Steve's cage was not fixed, nor was his snarled coat of wool tamed.

The following day, on my way home from a consulting appointment, I spotted something lying in the road ditch. Bedraggled, matted, no discernible movement. It was Steve.

I jumped out of the car and rushed to the prone form to check for signs of life. I was relieved to find him breathing and unharmed. It appeared Steve was merely playing possum, trying to pass unnoticed as he slowly worked his way back to his former home.

Nature has many camouflaging techniques: some animals have markings, colors, or other traits that help them blend into their surroundings to avoid being captured and eaten by predators. Steve, it seemed, had his own such skills. There was nothing Steve resembled as much as roadkill, and he made the most of it.

When he sensed no one was watching, Steve made steady progress, hopping southward along the road ditch. But as soon as he heard a car or human approach, he assumed his still-as-death impersonation, hoping he would be overlooked as routine roadside carnage rather than being apprehended and returned to his cage.

About this same time we unintentionally began a free-range rabbit-raising experiment. I had placed new grain feeders into some of the cages, one of which housed a mother rabbit with a litter of month-old babies. Each day when I fed them, one or two of the babies were gone. It wasn't until all eight of them had disappeared that I discovered the gap in the mouth of the feeder. The bunnies had to work hard to squeeze out of the gap, but they had managed it. Soon we began spotting them around the farm, dodging under a haystack or mower deck whenever we tried to catch them. These bunnies sometimes joined Steve in his wanderings.

In the coming weeks we frequently rescued Steve and his assorted companions from the nearby road ditches. But it was Steve who did most of the traveling. The free-range bunnies tended to stay near the farm, but not Steve. He preferred the open road. Sometimes his clever disguise rendered him as the likeness of a dead raccoon or a very small fox. Often a dead cat. He had perfected the art—he was roadkill extraordinaire.

When found out, Steve was terribly guilt-ridden. I think Steve was by nature a conformist. He would happily have lived out his days according to the rules, but he seemed driven by an overwhelming desire to return to his home and littermates in Starbuck. His escape attempts left him feeling horribly guilty and ashamed.

Over the next days, I made many temporary repairs to Steve's cage door. Each time, Steve figured out how to unlatch, unknot, or chew through the new challenge. Terry planned to build a new escape-proof cage for Steve—as soon as he found the time. Meanwhile, on our trips to and from town, Terry and I kept our eyes peeled, scanning the road ditches, watching for Steve.

We had always been viewed askance by our neighbors who were regular farmers, raising large herds of beef cattle and cultivating hundreds or even thousands of acres of corn, wheat, and soybeans. With raised eyebrows and puzzled looks, they watched us devote our time and small acreage to all types of odd species: llamas, alpacas, angora rabbits, and, as one neighbor put it, "them funny-lookin' little long-haired sheep."

And now, the regular appearance of Steve in the road ditches didn't help our image as serious farmers. Soon the word spread, and our neighbors, too, began to keep an eye out for the runaway rabbit. Leroy was kind enough to return Steve to us on two occasions.

Leroy was a man of few words. The first time he brought

Steve home, he drove his old truck into our yard and sat waiting in the cab until I approached.

"Hi, Leroy. What's up?" I asked.

Leroy stuck his grizzled head out the open window and said, "I got yer rabbit in the back."

He remained silent in the cab while I walked to the back of the truck. I made a quick visual sweep of the truck bed, looking for signs of Steve. Cluttered with the usual farmer's gear, the truck bed housed a chain saw, some dented oil and gasoline cans, heaps of tangled baler twine, part of what appeared to be a carburetor, several lengths of log chain, a few rusty tools, a sack of dog food, and three straw bales. It took me a while to spot Steve, but there he was, nearly indistinguishable from the discarded rag mophead atop the mound of baler twine.

"Thanks for bringing him home, Leroy," I said when I had Steve safely in my arms.

Leroy leaned his head slightly out the window and spat a stream of brown tobacco juice onto the gravel drive. He looked first at me and then at Steve. Wordlessly, Leroy adjusted the wad of chewing tobacco wedged beneath his lower lip and shook his head slowly. Though he said nothing, the expression on his face spoke eloquently, "I've seen some crazy things in my day, but this takes the cake."

Leroy started up his truck and slowly navigated back down the drive and out to the highway.

The second time Leroy brought Steve home, the encounter began as a replay of the first time. Leroy drove his old pickup into the yard and sat motionlessly in the cab until I approached. I stood waiting beside the driver's door while Leroy leisurely rolled down his window. When the wad of tobacco in his cheek was adjusted to his satisfaction, Leroy said, "I got yer rabbit."

I walked around to the rear of the truck and looked into the back, seeking signs of Steve. This time, the truck bed looked like a collision of the Bermuda Triangle and Area 51—a place into which all manner of things disappear, never to be seen again. Not surprisingly, Steve wasn't visible to the naked eye, so I climbed into the truck bed and began picking through the tangled mass of rubble. I spent a few minutes searching before Leroy called out gruffly, "He's up here. With me."

It was true. There sat Steve in the cab beside Leroy. I wrenched open the rusty passenger door. Simultaneously, Leroy and Steve turned their rumpled heads to face me—the disheveled rabbit with the guilty conscience, seated beside the stout old farmer in bib overalls and greasy seed corn cap.

Leroy reached over and patted Steve on his knotted head. Steve bore the unexpected display of affection with good grace before turning his head away in embarrassment.

In a rare burst of wordiness, Leroy told me how he had come upon the rabbit out on the highway. He described how Steve emerged from his deathlike state beside the road, rose to his feet, looked both ways, and began hopping tentatively across the pavement. Then, out of nowhere, a red sports car appeared over the hill. "Musta been some a them crazy people from the Cities," supposed Leroy. Before Steve was even halfway across the road the car was nearly upon him. Then, said Leroy, Steve sprang to life, running as if his life depended upon it. Which it probably did.

The rabbit ran like the wind, and as Leroy looked on helplessly, Steve narrowly escaped the wheels of the speeding car. A reluctant glimmer of admiration lit Leroy's eye as he looked over at Steve, still seated beside him on the ripped and stained upholstery. Steve's matted wool coat was nearly indistinguishable from the dirty cotton stuffing spilling out of the seat cushion.

The gnarled old man inclined his head and said, "That damn rabbit ain't much to look at, but by God, he's got gumption."

Ruth and Esther

The drought conditions continued into the fall. Other than the one torrential downpour that drenched Chris and Lamb Chop during county fair week, we had no more rain. After an all-too-brief greening up, the pasture grass dried up again, and we were facing a serious shortage of hay for winter.

Since mid-July the sheep had already been eating the hay that should have been saved for winter. Not only that, but our hay harvest that summer was less than half the usual amount. We normally cut hay in early June and again in July, and we often got a small third crop in August or early September. That year we got a good first crop, and then the rain stopped. There would be no second crop, and no third crop.

Hay became a scarce and valuable commodity. Prices rose sky-high, and semi-truck loads of hay came in from other states and down from Canada, selling for astronomical prices.

Earlier that summer, we picked out five nice ewe lambs to keep for breeding. Our plans were to sell the other lambs through ads in farm magazines, livestock breeders' journals, sheep shows, and other outlets for breeding stock for spinning-quality fleeces.

But with such poor pasture, Terry had already been forced to haul one livestock trailer of lambs to the auction barn to sell for slaughter. The drought conditions had not improved, and we found ourselves in mid-September with a dried-up pasture and not enough hay to bring our remaining sheep through the winter.

❋

One brisk fall morning, I stepped outside and was surprised to see Terry still at home. He had hitched the livestock trailer to his truck and was just closing the back door.

"Hey, I thought you were at work!" I said. "What are you doing home at this time of day, and where are you going with the livestock trailer?"

With a grim look on his face, Terry shot the bolt home and locked the trailer's tailgate and ramp into place. I realized that he had planned to have the trailer loaded up and gone before I came outside. He wanted to spare both of us another agonizing discussion about having to sell animals.

Terry walked around to the front, and I hopped up onto the running board and looked into the high-sided trailer. Inside were the five ewe lambs we had been planning to keep, all the remaining crossbred lambs, and three of our older purebred ewes. They were on their way to the auction barn to be sold for slaughter.

The lambs in the trailer were skittish and nervous, while the three older ewes looked up at me, their trusting eyes questioning this strange development. They were born on our farm and had never before seen the inside of a livestock trailer. I couldn't look them in the eye. I jumped to the ground and walked around the trailer to face Terry as he was securing the hitch to the truck.

He looked up at me for a second before returning his attention back to the hitch. He said, "We can't afford to feed 'em. They've got to go."

I climbed back onto the running board and again scanned the collection of sheep in the trailer. Fifteen sets of eyes returned my gaze. I looked over the fifteen beautiful fleeces in myriad shades from creamy white to golden brown to jet black. The spring lambs had the best fleeces—soft, clean, and brilliant in color, not yet faded by the sun. They had already grown about eight inches of soft wool. I could hardly bear to see them go. I couldn't even begin to think about the loss of the older ewes who had become far more than mere livestock.

I looked again in the trailer, certain I'd see Lamb Chop and Rambling Rose. Surely these two would be the first to go. Lamb Chop and Rose had very little commercial value, and in a business sense, they were a liability rather than an asset. It would be foolish to keep them when we were so short of hay.

"I know who you're looking for, but they're not in the trailer." Terry gestured over his shoulder to a corner of the sheep yard, where Lamb Chop and Whiplash stood by the fence. They were watching the activity around the trailer with interest, and nearby Rambling Rose lay curled up asleep in a patch of early morning sun.

Terry walked to the driver's side of the truck and slid inside without a word. It was clear Mr. Don't-Make-Pets-of-the-Livestock had no wish to discuss this serious lapse in judgment. "He must be getting soft in his old age," I said to Petey and Bart who stood beside me, eager to escort the truck and trailer out to the highway.

I felt huge relief when I realized Rambling Rose, Lamb Chop, and Whiplash would be spared, but at the same time I felt a small stab of betrayal. If Terry wasn't going to make those tough decisions, who would? If we continued to make

our business decisions based on sentiment, our enterprise
was doomed to fail, and before long we would have to sell all
of the animals.

I turned my attention back to the sheep in the trailer. Near
the back I spotted a familiar red fleece. It was Buck. I couldn't
bear to look any longer. I jumped down to the ground and
confronted Terry.

"Let me try to advertise again. That little black ram lamb
of Ada's isn't half bad," I said to Terry. "I know it's getting late
in the year, but maybe if we get a few of them listed in the
next issue of the journal, we can sell them as breeding stock,
and they won't have to go for slaughter. And we can keep Buck
for his wool."

"It's too late." Terry looked tired and discouraged. "We
won't have enough hay to keep any of them over winter if we
keep feeding the whole lot of them while we wait to advertise.
We don't have the hay to feed anyone but Lloyd and the ewes.
We can't keep any of this year's lambs." He continued to avoid
the topic of Rambling Rose, Lamb Chop, and Whiplash.

Rosie ambled over in our direction, bawling loudly to her
beloved Buck.

"I'm surprised you didn't load Rosie up with the rest of
them," I said. "If she has genetic issues, we really shouldn't
keep her."

"She's got to stay to take care of Rambling Rose," he said.
"Without Rosie and her bell, Rambling Rose would never
make it."

I wholeheartedly agreed, but I knew the day's actions
probably spelled the end of my shepherding career.

"Well, maybe we should shear those lambs, so we can at
least save the wool?" I suggested in yet another delaying tactic.

"No. I know it's a shame to waste the fleeces, but if they
have to go, let's make the trip as easy on them as possible,"
Terry said.

He was right. Shearing—especially a lamb's or yearling's first shearing—leaves the animal feeling naked and vulnerable, and it would make their trip far more stressful.

"Can you wait five minutes before you go?" I asked Terry. "I've got one more idea."

I went back into the house and called our friend Howard. A month earlier he had offered to buy a couple of lambs to be butchered for his own family's use. He was still interested. Howard offered a better price than we would get at the stockyard, and I was grateful.

Terry opened the back door of the trailer and pulled out Ruth and Esther, the two meatiest of the crossbred lambs. He herded them back inside the pasture gate and let them go. Ruth and Esther dashed away, kicking up their heels and jumping in the air, ecstatic at being set free.

Inside the trailer, all of the lambs were frightened. I knew what the trip would be like for them. I sometimes went with Terry when he hauled sheep to the auction barn. Their alarm would intensify when they reached the auction barn and stockyard, where the loud voices of the handlers would echo through the trailer. The lambs would be pulled from the trailer, then weighed, marked, and herded into a big, dusty corral. The glorious and magnificent Buck, whose future had once gleamed so brightly, would be sold for mere pennies to the dollar of his worth.

Raised on sunshine and green pastures, the confused and frightened Buck would be hustled up a ramp and herded into a vast holding pen. Buck's striking red fleece would disappear into a bawling sea of anonymous white feeder lambs on their way to slaughter, and he would be gone.

❊

We had come to realize that our dream—to breed and raise Shetland and Icelandic sheep to produce fine-quality wool for hand spinners —would depend on our salesmanship. Unfortunately, there isn't a ready commodity or livestock market where one can sell this type of sheep without extensive marketing. This wasn't the first autumn we had sent a truckload of animals to the slaughter market. All too often, our breeding and fleece-producing lambs had become "feeder lambs." It bothered me to know the lambs were slaughtered, and it also disturbed me to think that their beautiful fleeces were going to waste.

This time, I came up with a plan that would eliminate at least a part of that waste. When I spoke to Howard about the two lambs to be butchered, I asked him to save the hides of those lambs. Meanwhile, I would make arrangements with a man who made sheep hides into rugs. I'd seen examples of his work, and grisly though it may sound, he was a master at turning a fresh hide into a handsome lamb's wool rug.

The man's occupation was taxidermy, and he impressed upon me the importance of timeliness. It was an unseasonably hot September, and if left untreated, the fresh hides would start to decompose very quickly. To complicate matters further, the taxidermist was leaving shortly on a two-week hunting trip, so I had a very small window of opportunity to pick up the hides from the butcher and deliver them to the taxidermist to be scraped and treated before he left on vacation.

The lambs would be slaughtered at a butcher's shop the following morning, and the taxidermist needed the hides before four o'clock that afternoon. I would be working on a consulting job in Browns Valley that day, and I knew the timing would be tight for my task afterward. Throughout my day in Browns Valley I had thought about the two lambs and their appointment with destiny. I was not looking forward to gathering their lifeless pelts after the slaughter, but salvaging their hides seemed to make their deaths slightly less wasteful and pointless.

When my work in Browns Valley was finished, I gathered up my files, loaded them into the car, and headed toward home.

The road between Browns Valley and Wheaton, which skirts Lake Traverse on Minnesota's western border, is one of my favorite drives. Like much of Traverse County, this stretch of road is peaceful, largely undeveloped and unspoiled. The only thing that disturbs the serenity of this lovely drive is the wild turkeys. On my weekly trips to and from Browns Valley, I often spotted flocks of twenty to thirty of the big birds feeding on spilled grain and roadside vegetation.

These turkeys had some notoriety. One winter they had become so plentiful that Browns Valley city officials declared them a public nuisance and a health hazard. Heavy snows had covered the turkeys' usual feeding grounds, and the turkeys moved into town in search of food. Some houses soon had a dozen or more turkeys roosting on their roofs. But what began as an amusing curiosity soon became a real aggravation. The ammonia-rich turkey droppings took the paint off the houses' exterior walls and the hoods and roofs of cars. The hungry birds also accosted the citizens who were going about town minding their own business. After many citizen complaints, the city applied for a permit to eliminate the turkeys within the city limits.

Apparently the turkeys didn't harbor a grudge, because they didn't completely evacuate the area. They can still be found lurking around Browns Valley, though they now tend to congregate on the outskirts of town. And, on my weekly trips to a consulting job there, I usually encountered a flock of turkeys at a certain spot on the highway a few miles north of town. The turkeys showed little fear of my vehicle; they simply moved slowly off the highway while I waited.

But on that day, the throng was even slower than usual. As I sat idling in my car, the turkeys continued browsing in the ditches and walking back and forth across the road directly in front of my car. The novelty of watching the grazing turkeys wore off quickly, and I wanted to continue on my way. I had an appointment with the taxidermist, and I couldn't be late.

I honked the horn, but other than a few beady-eyed glances, it barely provoked a response. I shifted the car into drive and began to creep forward, the car's bumper nudging the birds. They stood their ground and refused to budge. They fluffed themselves out to twice their normal size and pecked belligerently at the bumper.

My camera was lying on the seat beside me, and I was tempted to use it. Its real purpose was to document evidence for my work on affordable housing programs: for example, I could photograph substandard workmanship to help settle disputes between contractors and property owners. But it also came in handy for opportunities like this. Not only would a picture of the turkey standoff provide future entertainment for me, it would prove that it had actually occurred. I could show my skeptical family that I really don't make these stories up. Due to client confidentiality, I couldn't disclose much about my work, but I did mention some memorable events. "I was attacked by a man with a knife today," I'd say. Or "I had a run-in with a flock of turkeys over by Lake Traverse today." Or "I was nearly run down by an old lady in a Buick today." But then I remembered my errand at the butcher shop. There was no time to capture that potentially prize-winning photograph.

Besides, I was afraid I'd end up like the star of the Alfred Hitchcock movie *The Birds*. I could just imagine myself being pecked to death and found lying at the side of the road. The story would make the front page of the weekly edition of the *Valley News*, but it just wouldn't be worth it.

I arrived home that afternoon with moments to spare. If I made good time I figured I could still transfer the hides from the butcher's shop, about half an hour from our farm, to the taxidermist's in Alexandria—another half-hour's drive. Terry had washed his hands of the whole sordid affair, so I was on my own.

The best vehicle for the job was undoubtedly Terry's truck, but because of its rundown condition, I didn't want to drive it through town at a very busy time of day. Then I imagined hauling the freshly butchered sheep's hides in my car. I jumped into the pickup and headed out.

I was speeding toward town when out of the corner of my eye I spotted a big fluffy cat, lying dead on the shoulder of the road. With relief I noticed it wasn't any of our own cats, but still, it was a shame to see any animal killed on the road.

"Poor kitty. What an awful way to go," I thought. As I accelerated past the lifeless form, I noticed the poor animal's fur was matted. "I can't understand why people don't take better care of their pets," I said to myself.

"Hey, wait a minute!" The brakes squealed and the old truck swerved crazily before coming to a shuddering halt. Grinding roughly through the gears, I found reverse and roared backward toward the prone figure.

It was Steve doing his roadkill impersonation. He did a remarkable job of it. He lay still as death, a slight breeze ruffling the feathery wool at his ear tips. His eyes were tightly closed. The only improvement he could have made to his disguise would have been to simulate tire tread marks over his body. I wound down the truck's window and leaned out to get a better look.

"Steve! Stop it this instant!" My voice—honed by two decades of motherhood—worked its magic. One eye opened ever so slightly.

I yelled out the window, "Go home! For heaven's sake, Steve! I don't have time for this today."

Steve did not respond. He squeezed his eyes more tightly shut and tried to make himself appear flatter.

I climbed out of the truck and approached Steve. "This is great! Just great! Why did you have to pick today to pull one of your stunts? I'm running late already." I carried Steve to the

truck and plopped him down on the seat beside me. Like it
or not, he would have to join me on my errand to the butcher
shop and taxidermist.

Eager to make up some lost time, I accelerated the rickety
pickup to near seventy. Shaking, shuddering, and bouncing
along, the pickup struggled to meet the demands being made
so unexpectedly upon it. In addition to the bald tires, worn-
out shocks, and rusted body, the steering on the old truck
wasn't very reliable, either. When we careened around the
curves, I reached over with my free hand to pin Steve down,
so that he didn't fly off the seat.

We arrived at the butcher's shop in record time. I walked
into the shop, where I had hoped to find a tidy bundle of wool
attached to a cleanly scraped hide. But no such luck. When I
asked the woman at the counter about the hides, she pointed
toward a dark corner of the shop, where a bloody mass of
wool was piled high in a cardboard box.

The box was huge and overflowing. I cautiously picked
it up and staggered out the door of the shop. The bottom of
the box was apparently soaked through with blood, because
it gave way explosively in my arms on my way to the truck,
spilling the grisly remains of Ruth and Esther onto the gravel
parking lot.

I dropped to my hands and knees and gathered up the
slippery, bloody masses of hide and wool, stuffing them back
into what was left of the cardboard box. By the time I got the
whole mess loaded into the truck, I was liberally covered in
gravel, blood, and long, moist strips of sinewy tissue.

When I climbed back into the cab, Steve averted his eyes, as
if disgusted by my appearance. "Get over it. You're way too sensitive," I snapped. I was in no mood for his disapproving looks.

As we bounced and swerved our way toward Alexandria,
I glanced at my watch. If we hurried, we could still get to the
taxidermist's by the four o'clock deadline. But there was one

important element I had not taken into consideration—the pickup's advanced state of deterioration. It had done a valiant job so far today, but it now seemed to have completely run out of steam.

The pickup coughed, sputtered, jerked, and finally stalled. After several attempts, I managed to start it again, but after that it merely limped along. Finally, we neared the shop in Alexandria, where I stopped impatiently for a series of red lights. At the third stoplight, I checked my watch again. Time was running out. When the light turned green, in my haste I popped the clutch too quickly, and the pickup stalled once again, rolling into the middle of a busy intersection.

All around me, car horns blared. I twisted the key in the ignition, then pumped the gas pedal and twisted the key again. It was no use. The truck was going nowhere.

I looked up and noticed a police car approaching. It was at that point I became keenly aware of my situation. I was stalled in the middle of a busy intersection, my hands and clothing smeared with blood, transporting a bundle of carnage. I glanced into the rearview mirror and noticed a piece of sinew dangling from my nose.

Beside me sat Steve, riding shotgun. Though I was completely innocent of any crime, I didn't want to explain this to anyone in a uniform.

-*-

Against all odds, Steve and I were spared incarceration that day, and the remains of Ruth and Esther arrived at the taxidermist's shop just in time. The two sheep were transformed into a pair of soft, creamy-colored rugs.

The rugs turned out well, and Terry and I briefly considered adding tanned sheepskins to our list of products for sale on our future website. But I just couldn't convince myself to go through that ordeal again.

Conclusion

The year was drawing to a close, and we began in earnest to prepare for winter. The sheep, llamas, and Tony were all reunited in the main pasture, where they could share the warmth and protection of the shed.

Mack Dawg, whose raging hormones eventually ebbed to mere smoldering embers, rejoined the flock as its official guardian. It looked like he might become an effective guard llama. Camilla and the sheep were far from pleased to see Mack again, but in time they became resigned to his presence.

The drought ended in late September with a solid week of soaking rains. Though it was too late in the year to revive the pasture or the hay crop, we looked forward to a green spring and hoped for a better year ahead.

The breeding of our ewes was complete. Ragnar had been mated with some of our Icelandic crossbred ewes, but Lloyd managed the lion's share of the work. Mary took Ragnar to her farm for the rest of the fall and winter. He was having the time of his life flaunting himself before a new harem of ewes. Lloyd was haggard and thin—a shadow of his former self—which is typical of a ram at the tail end of the breeding season.

It had been a year since I began my short-lived career as a full-time shepherdess. Four months later Terry had issued his ultimatum, and he and I had agreed if we didn't show a profit by the end of the year, we would sell most of the livestock, keeping only one or two sheep to provide wool for my own spinning. I would return to a full-time job in town.

The time had come to determine the fate of our flock. On that November evening Terry once again sat down at the kitchen table with a pile of receipts and bank statements. I worked at the spinning wheel, but rather than being soothed by the repetitive motion, I was on edge, waiting for the verdict. Deep down, we both knew it had not been a good year financially, but we wished with all our hearts that Terry's findings would be positive.

As Terry added his columns of figures, I thought back on the events of the past year. It had been nearly eight months since I really started in earnest with the grant writing business. At first I'd been devastated to learn I couldn't continue my quiet life as a full-time shepherdess. But by the fall I felt almost reluctant to think of abandoning the growing consulting business that I had worked so hard to establish.

Though the family, farm, and animals were my passion and priority, the consulting business, too, had become more than just a stopgap measure. Developing projects and seeing them come to fruition was almost as rewarding, in its own way, as shepherding.

If I were to return to full-time shepherding, I knew I would miss my small-town clients. In the past I'd worked with bigger, more professionally staffed clients. These clients were efficient, well trained, and experienced in dealing with grant programs. But in the past year I'd learned that I really liked working with small towns—those communities where the city office was closed for a week while the clerk stayed home to care for her grandchildren who had all come down with the croup. Or where the city council met late at night in the fall, because most of the council members were helping with the harvest. Those were the kinds of places I liked to work. Places where real life still took precedence over policies, procedures, and Robert's Rules of Order.

Finally, Terry looked up from his spreadsheets and said, "Well, there's good news and bad news. The good news is we made a profit of $24.16. But the bad news is that's before counting depreciation on the machinery, which will put us back in the hole."

The angora rabbits were the only part of the entire farm operation that showed a net profit that year. It was quite a nice profit, too, totaling thousands of dollars. The rabbits were relatively inexpensive to feed, house, and care for, and their wool brought in the highest price per ounce.

All other aspects of the farm showed a financial loss. The sheep, llamas, alpaca, and Terry's small grain harvest—all appeared under the net loss column. Even the profit realized from the angora wool barely offset it.

Terry and I sat together and stared at the rows of figures, willing them to change, willing them to show a decent profit, just enough to let us keep our bargain with ourselves and allow us to continue with the animals and the farm.

After a long while, Terry cleared his throat and said, "Well, it *was* an especially bad year. For everyone, I mean, I doubt many farmers made a profit this year. The drought cost us most of our hay crop, and it nearly ruined the pasture."

Catching the drift of his thoughts, I added, "And I didn't do nearly as much marketing as I should have. I ended up spending so much time on the grant writing I just didn't have time to do the website, and I only worked a few fiber shows."

"On the bright side," said Terry, "the consulting profits are healthy."

"I'd love to be a full-time shepherdess." I said to Terry. "But the part-time consulting business isn't so bad. Maybe it doesn't have to be all or nothing."

We looked into each other's eyes for a long moment, neither wanting to admit defeat. Terry finally broke the silence. "What do you say to giving the farm another year?"

"That works for me," I said.

Terry pushed his chair away from the table, stood up, and decisively stuffed the hundreds of crumpled receipts into a big brown envelope. He wadded up the financial statement he had prepared and ceremoniously tossed it into the trash.

We put on our hats, coats, and gloves and headed outside together to do the evening chores. Though I was pleased our decision did not force us to sell the animals or give up the fiber business, I wondered if we had failed ourselves by not sticking to our bargain. Conflicting emotions warred within me as we walked from the house to the sheep shed.

But that old feeling of euphoria could not be stifled. I resolved again to start a website and do a better job of marketing both the breeding stock and the wool products next year. By the time we reached the sheep shed, my spirits were soaring again. I punched Terry on the shoulder and yelled, "We're in business for another year!"

Keeping watch

One November evening Chris was in a panic. He was packing his bags for the overnight field trip his class was taking the following day. As usual, he left it all until the last minute. He had each of us rushing through the house in search of clean socks, shoes, notebooks, and other required items. It was nearly midnight when we fell wearily into bed.

It seemed we had just fallen asleep when once again we woke to the dogs barking in response to the yip of distant coyotes. Terry opened his eyes and groaned. "I'd better go out and check the sheep."

"Oh, I'm sure they're all safe in the shed." I had just drifted off to sleep, and I didn't care to be dragged fully back to consciousness due to some minor uprising among the omnipresent coyotes. "From the sound of it, the coyotes are way back in the hills. I don't think they're going to bother the sheep tonight."

Just as reluctant to be awakened as I, Terry grunted in assent and rolled over, and we both fell asleep again.

The coyotes had been less troublesome since the drought ended, and we had begun to leave the door to the sheep shed partially open at night for ventilation. There were no young lambs to worry about, and Mack seemed to be doing his job as guardian. And even though the door was ajar, the sheep, llamas, and alpaca always made their way back to the shed at dusk and stayed there until daylight.

The shrill sound of the alarm woke us early the next morning. Chris needed to be at school by six o'clock—before the school bus—to catch a ride for his field trip. So, on that chilly morning shortly before dawn, Chris and I were in the car headed for town.

The car's headlights swept over the far pasture as we rounded the final curve in the driveway. Illuminated by the headlights, a group of dark forms was visible dotting the hillside.

"Look!" I said as I stepped on the brake. I stopped the car for a moment while Chris and I marveled at the rare sight.

The sheep were lying out on a hillside as if they had spent the night outside. Forming a protective outer ring around the sheep were the larger forms of Mack, Camilla, and Tony.

Judging from what Chris and I saw that morning, the sheep had actually spent the night outside under the stars. That would be a first. An uneasy feeling swept over me as I remembered the howl of coyotes and my suggestion to Terry that he not bother to go out and check the sheep.

When I returned home after dropping Chris at school, I parked the car in the garage, then walked out to the far pasture to see if I could learn what had caused this unusual phenomenon.

On a normal day, one of my favorite tasks is walking out to the far pasture early in the morning to check on the flock. But on that particular morning I took no time to admire the sunrise through the mist. I was concerned about the flock's astonishing decision to spend the night outdoors.

The sun was peeking over the treetops when I reached the hillside where Chris and I had spotted the flock earlier. The animals were just rising, stretching their legs and shaking out their fleeces after a long, cold night. Mack, Camilla, and Tony were all on their feet, yawning hugely. The ewes began to rise and move about. I walked among them, calling their names and patting their heads as I passed. I saw the solid rusty-colored mound of Rosie still lying down, and beside her the small bump of her lamb. I reached out to tweak Rosie's ear when Tony thrust his face directly in my path.

"What are you doing out here?" I asked Tony. "Were you outside all night?"

His responding *Hmmm* went unnoticed as I came to a sudden stop. There beside Rosie lay Rambling Rose's body, lifeless on the grass.

Vividly surreal, as if in a dream, that moment is burned in my memory. The watery, early morning sunlight breaking through the trees, the brittle stems of grass where I knelt, the springy whorls of soft wool curling around Rambling Rose's face, wet with dew.

Rambling Rose looked as if she were simply asleep. Her face was relaxed and calm, and I knew that never again would she rush headlong in a blind panic, frantically chasing the elusive jangle of her mother's bell.

At last, Rambling Rose had achieved her heart's desire. She lay peaceful and serene beside Rosie, and I like to think that's how she entered eternity—with her last conscious moment nestled beside old mother of-the-year Rosie. Safe and secure, with the flock surrounding them protectively.

Rosie, chewing her cud and gazing off into the distance, remained steadfast beside the small lifeless body. The rest of the flock stood nearby, just beginning to stir and move about in the early morning sun.

I looked around for signs of a coyote attack or other disturbance. The pasture grass had been trampled and flattened in an area circling the spot where Rose lay. But the body of Rambling Rose was unmarked. I knelt again to examine her, and I could see that she hadn't been touched by coyotes or trampled by sheep. She seemed to have died of natural causes, falling victim at last to the congenital imperfections that had troubled her since birth.

As I lifted Rose's body to carry her home, I noted the signs that the entire flock had spent the night outside. The outer ring of the trampled circle was churned up and muddy from the llamas' feet, and I wondered if they had cause to defend the flock against coyotes, or if they had simply chosen to stay awake through the night, pacing and watching for danger.

I could imagine what had happened. Like a well-oiled machine, the individual members of the flock had worked together to keep the savage coyotes away from Rose in her last hours. Mack and Camilla patrolled the perimeter. The sheep formed a tight impregnable circle with Rosie and her dying lamb at the center. Looking at the evidence, it was clear: the flock had stayed outside all night, encircling and keeping vigil over the still, small form of Rambling Rose.

Cradling the lifeless body in my arms, I began the long walk toward home. Rosie trudged quietly in my wake, while the rest of the flock looked after us. They dropped their heads as if they would remain in the far pasture to begin their day's grazing.

But after turning the first corner by the big oak tree, nearly halfway home, I heard footsteps behind me. I stopped for a moment, and then I was surrounded. Mack, Camilla, Tony and Whiplash, Lamb Chop, and the whole dysfunctional crew were there. The flock had come through for Rambling Rose in her final hour, and they were escorting her body home.

-*-

As the days passed, life returned to normal for the family and the flock. Terry resumed his habit of going out at dusk every night to make sure everyone was safely in the shed before nightfall.

For about a week after the death of Rambling Rose, Rosie continued her nightly custom of calling for her daughter when the flock returned to the shed in the evening. Eventually even that ritual ceased, and there was no tangible evidence the blind lamb had ever existed.

The life and death of Rambling Rose made a lasting impression on all of us. I realize that, despite their rude manners, the animals may have more decency than I've ever given them credit for. Rambling Rose—the one who was least among them—brought out the courage and loyalty of the flock when it mattered most.

But then again, maybe I'm reading too much into it. Maybe it was just a coincidence, and I should do as Jon so often advises, "Mom, don't psychoanalyze. They're sheep. Just throw a little hay in there and walk away."

Still, whenever I am tempted to complain about the rude, inconsiderate nature of sheep, I remember that cold dark night when the flock lay together on the windswept hillside, keeping watch.

Epilogue

Lamb Chop was our first bottle lamb. With time and experience we've become better able to care for orphaned and abandoned lambs. We keep a supply of sheep colostrum on hand during the lambing season. We learned that healthy bottle lambs can survive nicely in the sheep shed when they are kept warm and enclosed to prevent injuries. It's best for lambs to know right from the start they are sheep, and they belong with other sheep.

Lamb Chop is now well adjusted and happy as a member of the flock. Though she was abandoned by her mother at birth, Lamb Chop herself is an excellent mother. She has given birth four times, bearing two single lambs and two sets of twins.

We have some great memories of Lamb Chop's days in our midst. Even though she is now a regular member of the flock, Lamb Chop has retained her affinity for both human and canine companionship. She loves people, and a fast car on the driveway still catches her eye.

Grouchy old Rosie is still with us, and she is now well into her twilight years. She no longer produces either lambs or fleeces, but she stubbornly lives on. Her raspy voice is almost totally gone, due to more than a decade of constant complaining.

For now, it appears that Steve's traveling days are over. His cage was repaired before winter set in, and he was forced to abandon his quest to return to Starbuck. His quizzical glances have lately been directed toward Louise, who lives in the cage next door.

The sterilization of Mack Dawg put a kink in his rampaging lifestyle, but it didn't totally solve the problem. Though he has not gone completely berserk again, Mack's arrogant attitude resurfaced, just as his wool and toenails grew back.

If Mr. and Mrs. Tinkles were capable of permanently retiring to their Create-Your-Own-Castle and shutting out all of humanity, I believe they would gladly raise the drawbridge once and for all, flood the moat, and consign the rest of the household to the fires of hell. But as it is, they can't retreat from reality. Their preferred source of drinking water is the toilet bowl, and the Friskies are dispensed (far too sparingly, in the Tinkleses' opinion) by Chris into a bowl on top of the dryer in the basement. So they continue to tolerate our presence for the time being.

And as for Tux . . . well, what can one say? Luan still faithfully cares for him with an ever-expanding arsenal of homeopathic and herbal remedies, still seeking some magic antidote to soothe the untamed beast that is Tux.

ACKNOWLEDGMENTS

Our lives here on the farm are often chaotic, and summers especially are a disorganized jumble of events and experiences. In some of this book's passages, the dates or sequencing of events have been altered for clarity and simplicity. Some names and identifying details have been changed to protect the privacy of individuals and small communities, and the stories reflect my own memories of events. Not all of the animals pictured are mentioned in the book. Some of the photos include images of animals that came along after the book was written.

This book tells about our experiences with a small-scale livestock operation that is supported by our off-the-farm jobs. Because our livelihood doesn't depend entirely on our farm income, we've gotten away with doing some crazy things and making poor business decisions, such as supporting a bunch of geriatric sheep geezers long after their productive years are over. I feel fortunate to be able to do things that full-time farmers don't often have the luxury to do. Many of our friends and neighbors run full-time farming operations with expertise and efforts that far exceed ours. Theirs are the truly remarkable stories.

I would like to express my gratitude and thanks to the following people.

The skillful and good-humored Ann Regan, editor-in-chief at Borealis Books, who guided the manuscript through the publication process from beginning to end. Managing editor Shannon Pennefeather as well as Alison Aten and Mary Poggione in marketing, copyeditor Mindy Keskinen, the designers, and everyone else who worked on the book. You've done a great job.

Luan, Mary, and the other friends and neighbors who are mentioned in the book, and also those of you who are not mentioned by name but who enrich our lives with your friendship.

Dan Hartsell of Country Vet in Alexandria. One of Dan's best attributes is his willingness to attempt a cure, even for the most ill, exotic, or berserk patient. He has performed some spectacular procedures on our animals. Dan has brought Lazarus the alpaca back from the brink of death more than once, using a unique combination of horse pills, hog tonic, and a good dose of black magic.

The city clerks, mayors, council members, and nonprofit agencies who took a chance on hiring a shepherdess–grant writer: Thank you for providing me with jobs and projects over the years. It's been a pleasure working with you.

I have to acknowledge specifically the city of Browns Valley, Minnesota. Browns Valley was one of my very first consulting clients. The city council and staff, as well as the town's people, have left a lasting impression. And this list would not be complete without a mention of Browns Valley's flood recovery task force and those memorable deal-or-no-deal road trips with the state agencies.

And, of course, the animals. The sheep, cats, dogs, llamas, alpacas, and rabbits: faithful companions along the way (some more faithful than others) without whom life would be a whole lot less interesting. Despite what others may say, I know you are beings of great depth, complexity, and understanding.

Terry, for his good nature and good heart, not to mention his strong back. Terry is the ideal partner for the dual enterprises of farming and life in general. He's the one with the common sense and the level head—the glue that holds it all together. Terry's willingness to participate in all of these animal projects goes well beyond the call of duty, and I'm always amazed at his incredible patience and grace in coping with the unexpected.

Beth, Jeremy, Jon, and Chris, for their encouragement and inspiration. Thanks for being such good sports about your inclusion in this memoir. These four have dispensed advice, developed a website, fixed my computer, made jokes, and critiqued the manuscript (as well as my parenting skills and fashion sense). I'm certain it's a better book and I'm a better person for it. Really.

And finally, grandsons Kaiden and Ryder, for the opportunity to experience the blessings and wonder of creation all over again.